WINNING THE ERP GAME

A Coaching Guide to Packaged Application Business Success

DAVID STEFANICK

STX Consulting
2020

First Printing: 2020

ISBN 978-0-578-65496-6

Published by STX Consulting, LLC
1604 Cedar Lane, Raleigh, NC 27614

www.STXConsulting.com/Publishing

Limit of Liability/Disclaimer of Warranty: While the author has used his best efforts in preparing this book, he makes no representation or warranties with respect to the accuracy or completeness of the contents of this book and specifically disclaim any implied warranties of merchantability or fitness for a particular purpose. No warranty may be created or extended by sales representatives or written sales materials. The advice and strategies contained herein may not be suitable for your situation. You should consult with a professional where appropriate. Neither the publisher or the author shall be liable for any loss of profit or any other commercial damages, including but not limited to special, incidental, consequential, or other damages.

Library of Congress Control Number: 2020904194

Trademark Acknowledgements: The following are registered trademarks in the Unites States of America and other countries.

SAP, S4 HANA, HANA, ASAP, Activate, ECC, R/3, SAPPHIRE, Oracle, AIM, Siebel, Infor, Infor Deployment Method, Microsoft, Microsoft Dynamics Sure Step Methodology Microsoft Teams, Excel, PowerPoint, Workday, Salesforce, ServiceNow, Celonis, Celonis Intelligent Business Cloud, Tableau, Qlik, Splunk, Slack, Zoom, Webex, YouTube, ASUG, SUGEN, DSAG, Gartner, APQC, PCF, Apptio

This book is dedicated to my family. To my parents, my brothers, my sons, Michael and David, who have brought me much joy, and most importantly, to the love of my life and my best friend, my wife, Kathleen.

Contents

Acknowledgements

I would like to thank the following individuals who helped with input and/or reviewing my book. Having each of them share their industry knowledge, insight and experience is greatly appreciated and they are a great sounding board. I also want to thank Karen Celentano for her great input on the cover design.

Dr. Marianne Bradford (North Carolina State University)

Scott Chitty (Celonis)

Chris Cornett (Aloi Materials Handling and Automation)

John "Wes" Dyke (Caterpillar, Inc)

David Hofmeister (Champion Home Exteriors)

Heinz Schroeder (IBM-retired)

Greg Shumaker (Business Performance Integrated)

Sven Viehrig (IBM-retired)

Chapter 1 - Introduction and Background

"If you don't play to win, don't play at all."
Tom Brady, 6 Time Super Bowl Champion.

A quick internet search on failed ERP projects will return some sobering results. A number of industry surveys indicate that it is not that unusual for these projects to not meet expectations. One recent survey indicates that greater than 70% of business managers believed that their Enterprise Resource Planning (ERP) projects did not deliver the benefits expected.

I was recently engaged by a customer to help with some process improvements on an ERP implementation that they had been using for a number of years. While meeting with the customer, the founder and CEO of the company shared a story about his many business challenges and then asked me, "Are we the only ones struggling with getting value out of our ERP package investment?" My immediate answer was, "Absolutely not. If it's any consolation, you are not alone and there are actually a large number of companies who feel that way."

Budgets overrun while packaged software implementations do not meet the business expectation is an all too common theme. What customers receive versus what they expect has been a large delta. Why is it that most ERP project and large packaged application rollouts often miss the mark? My goal is to try and help answer this question and offer insight into how to hit the target and excel.

(Note: For purposes of this book, the term packaged application software means commercial off the shelf software that typically can be set up to provide one or several key processes for business transformation, e.g., SAP Enterprise Resource Planning (ERP), Salesforce Customer Relationship Management (CRM), Workday Human Capital Management (HCM), ServiceNow Information Technology Service Management (ITSM). Many packaged applications are available through the cloud as a Software as a Service (SaaS) offering.)

Your business needs to win big and outpace your competition in satisfying customers! Everybody wants to be a winner and be on a winning team. We all want our business team to share the feelings of emotion you see on the faces of the players and coaches that win a Championship or National Title. The overwhelming sense of accomplishment that results from proper preparation and hard work and achieving the ultimate goal. Successful teams have their roots in excellent leadership and governance with coaching and organizational management making timely and critical decisions. From assembling the team with the right players to motivating them to succeed to keeping the ownership engaged and committed. Likewise, a successful Enterprise Resource Planning deployment has its roots in much of the same characteristics. "All In" is a mantra and rallying cry not only for elite sports teams but it also applies to the business teams assembled to deliver ERP or any significant packaged application effort. The pride and motivation that your team gains from "winning the game" can serve as a basis to sustaining that high level of performance and keeping the business "in the zone" to achieve significant on-going business advantage and operational excellence.

ERP transformation projects are pervasive across the business world and have been around for over 30 years. With the emergence of SAP, Oracle, Infor and other key suppliers who have been synonymous with this space, we have seen the industry grow into one that every business uses in some form to run its operations. Bursting onto the scene back in the early 90's and ramping into the Year 2000 to address the much-hyped Y2K challenge, these efforts have taken on a life of their own. With often massive amounts of funding and business sweat applied to these initiatives, businesses attempt to implement and operate these complex solutions. Given the history and noted number of project failures, there are skeptics across most businesses. Imagine turning these naysayers into cheerleaders if these solutions went in faster, smoother and exceeded the business goals. You and your team might enjoy your own metaphoric ticker tape parade in New York City!

There are many factors that go into the playbook of implementing and operating an ERP package. One hears about (1) organizational change management, since ERP projects involve and impact many people on many fronts. It also includes (2) business process transformation and (3) technology associated with the software package and its implementation. All three are key pillars to underpin a successful project. However, within each of these pillars there is a dimension which warrants more emphasis in order to achieve and exceed expectations, governance.

Governance is a key ingredient for both information technology (IT) and business and is vital to your success. Effective governance is a secret sauce to winning and assures transparency and accountability. We will share more insight about ERP governance examples throughout the book but first we will add some clarity to the topic.

Everyone hears the term governance and it generates many different thoughts of what it means. We will frame what governance is important, especially as it pertains to ERP projects. Is it the executive champion and sponsor who is working behind the scenes to set the stage across the business? Is it the executive steering committee providing the support to overcome the inherent resistance to change? Is it the ERP program management office managing the program strategy, scope and change requests or the project team dealing effectively with the day to day tasks and issues? What about the business process owners and super users and their buy-in? These elements and much more are part of the broader ERP governance that needs to be indoctrinated and coached into the business culture as routine for ERP or other packaged applications to realize success. Many of the errors, fumbles and turnovers in past unsuccessful ERP packaged application projects can be traced directly to poor governance. For example, when business adoption is met with significant resistance, who will step up, acknowledge there is a major issue and press the right buttons. It could be largely a result of poor organizational change management efforts, but governance oversight can help uncover and identify the signs and make sure that a resolution plan is put in place and executed.

There is plenty already written about and many books covering packaged application software selection, module implementation and general use. My focus will be on addressing challenges to packaged application value realization, satisfying business expectations and achieving operational excellence. The term "value realization" means extracting the value and benefits from the implemented packaged application solution. Operational excellence is the execution of your business strategy more consistently and reliably than your competition as is evidenced by the results.

Within this book I share gained insight, lessons learned and Best Practices, augmenting packaged application supplier standard methodologies. The storyline will cut across all three pillars of transformation: people/culture, processes and technology, with an emphasis on governance. By synthesizing the guidelines outlined in this book across your project implementation life cycle and methodology, the aim is to help to improve the batting averages for ERP and other packaged application projects in achieving expectations. Whether you are a small, medium or large business, just starting a project, in the middle of a project or already live and running your ERP or packaged application, the insight can serve as a "timeout" moment for you to rally your team.

Many of the challenges of packaged application projects and their related competitive demands have parallels with team sports. The use of sports analogies and metaphors have been exercised throughout the pages. I use the term "Coaching Moment" to highlight lessons learned throughout the book. The hope is for you to leverage this coaching to increase the likelihood of you being the hero and driving in the winning run in the bottom of the ninth and not to go down swinging. Let's avoid reliving Casey's woes of no joy in Mudville.

Coincidentally, and related to sports metaphors, the NBA, NHL and FIFA professional sports organizations are significant users of ERP software. An NBA executive helped tip off a recent SAP SAPPHIRE customer event Keynote session with their own customer packaged application story. The fact that professional sports franchises are using ERP reinforces how pervasive these packages have become across all businesses and industries around the globe.

Why do so many ERP Projects Fail to Deliver on Expectations?

Among other things, ERP projects are complex, hard work and not easy! Acknowledge and communicate this message and plan for it. These projects often encompass many company processes, including differentiating processes with many nuances to them. Industries also have varying government requirements from tax compliance to Food and Drug Administration compliance. Add in the complexities of diverse corporate culture by country, region, company, employees and contractors, and one can see how the complexities stack up. There are the general dynamics of the business world that happen while the projects are underway, such as mergers, acquisitions and divestitures. New products or processes get introduced as well. I led one very complex global transformation that while in the middle of the realization phase, we got short notice to accommodate a major multi-billion-dollar business divestiture. A NASCAR analogy emerged of changing the oil on Dale Earnhardt Jr's car while he was going around the track at 200mph! It was incredibly challenging to have to plan to spin off a division representing a large piece of the business whose processes and data were intertwined within the remaining business while also moving forward with a global transformation rollout.

Troubled projects happen at good companies too not just poorly run companies! Sure, poorly run companies are at a higher risk, but bad things happen to good companies too! Just attend an ERP Users Group conference and you will hear from iconic brands who are or have struggled with some packaged software implementation.

The upside is these packaged application transformation projects hold immense potential benefit for companies to run their business processes and have become a "cost of admission" in order to compete. Many companies are realizing enormous value from these applications today and using them to propel their businesses to even greater value realization and success.

Getting Started - Value Assessment and Business Case

As you embark on a major ERP or packaged application business transformation, a typical first step (and Best Practice) prior to package selection, involves developing the **value assessment** and **business case**. The classic "burning platform" or objective(s) which is aligned with the enterprise strategy. The business case should contain the elements that define your success.

Integral to all transformation projects is the development of new business processes, the technology required and the people and business culture that needs to be transformed from the current "as-is" to the "to-be" to achieve the objectives. The value assessment and business case are critical activities and lay the foundation for everything that follows. It reflects high level business requirements and associated return on investment (ROI). I have been engaged on a significant number of projects that are deeply into the "how" aspects of the implementation without a value assessment or business case in place to first answer the "why are we as a business doing this"? When project team members are asked "why are you doing this project?", it is not unusual to hear them say, "we were told to put this in". This is typically the result of teams trying to shortcut the effort or avoid investing in the upfront costs of developing a business case. This is a giant mistake. You are not just putting in an ERP information technology (IT) project. You should be aligning your business strategy with developing the business requirements for your ERP project. Without a value assessment and business case, the likelihood is the ERP or packaged application project won't become fully aligned with your enterprise strategy. These projects will live on with significant on-going costs and by aligning them early on with your strategy the likelihood that they stay aligned with the business strategy increases significantly. Your business stakeholders should view this packaged application project as part of the engine to drive the on-going success of the business and not as a "turn it on and walk away" investment.

It is often unclear how ERP projects are started without some level of documented business case or value assessment. One client team suggested that either through IT consolidation or merger and acquisition, some IT harmonization onto a common ERP project is obviously required, so why go through the time, effort and cost of developing a business case and value assessment. I can assuredly state that the several weeks of upfront investment to define the business case and expected benefits are well worth it and will likely open windows into opportunities and strategic alignment that would have been missed.

Coaching Moment – Just like sports teams don't rush into the regular season, your business shouldn't just rush into the implementation project. Preseason preparation is part of the sports team's effort to assess the team and align it to the strategy for execution.

Before embarking on an ERP or any packaged application project, some level of value assessment and business case should be completed. Depending on the size of the initiative, at a minimum, carve out two to four weeks to engage in a value assessment and business case. With this baseline, you can align the initiative better

to the enterprise strategy and establish the metrics to quantify and qualify the implementation and on-going success of your project.

Packaged applications are everywhere in your business application landscape (Figure 1) and their footprint is growing. At the end of the day, the measure of how successful your packaged application solution is, should be quantified against the value assessment and business case. Business cases usually include benefits over a number of years after go-live. The sustainment team (also known as the Center of Excellence (CoE) team), which we will discuss in detail later, is normally responsible for monitoring and measuring the value realization after go-live in collaboration with the business executives who committed to the business case. This is one of many responsibilities the sustainment team should undertake as a Best Practice as the team responsible for the post go-live sustainment of the ERP solution.

Enterprise Application Landscape Example

Figure 1- Enterprise Application Landscape Example

Governance

The need for governance applies to the entire packaged application program across process, technology and organization. How are the right data and information gathered, presented, monitored and decisions made? Some areas are more visible and easily analyzed while others may lurk in the dark only to raise their head during the go-live or post go-live phases. For instance, if master data or performance is not governed effectively within an ERP rollout, the project may run into the wall. Massive master data conversion requirements that arrive late to the game may result in the team scrambling to then get these addressed. With performance, it can be as straight forward as transactions are just too slow for the user experience or, what previously was processed in the legacy system, takes much longer to process in the new solution. No proof of concept was part of the plan or worse, was removed from the plan to meet a delivery date, and it is not until go-live that users get any feel for what is being delivered.

Within the chapters of this book, I will elaborate on the pillars of packaged application transformation: organizational change management, business processes and technology. I will share lessons learned and examples on how to improve your efforts, emphasizing effective governance and innovative coaching. This can enable a successful project, achieving greater value and exceeding business expectations. This guidance can help you and your team not only "win the game" but enjoy winning at elite performance levels for years to come.

Next, let's introduce the players on the team.

Chapter 2 - The Team

"We must all hang together or most assuredly we will all hang separately."

Benjamin Franklin at the signing of the Declaration of Independence

Teams are made up of individual people in many different roles that join together to operate as one to achieve a goal. Most professional sports teams are comprised of the people you see perform during the game, e.g., the head coach, assistant coaches, players and team captains, trainers, and those you don't see such as those who plan and oversee the organization, e.g., the Owner, General Manager, Directors of Player Development/Evaluation/Scouting/Sports Science & Performance and other roles. Likewise, your team is comprised of different roles and responsibilities within its team structure. In a small to mid- size company without the luxury of a large team of players, it is common to have a few team members who wear multiple hats and play several roles with multiple responsibilities.

As part of the initial planning, the team structure is put into place. The team size and number of individuals is dependent on the size of the effort, the scope and your organization. This structure is critical as it creates the governing and executing bodies. Like any team, assembling the players and people who govern the team is vital. Without the right players, your team will not be successful and unlike the NBA, NFL, MLB, NHL, MLS and other professional teams, there is no "wait til next year" cliché to rally around. You will have to live with any resulting project mistakes that this team puts into place.

A typical packaged application implementation team is comprised of the customer team, and external teams from the software application supplier(s) and a very experienced systems integrator. These internal and external teams should come together to operate as one project implementation team to deliver a successful project. This chapter will focus largely on the internal customer team with a quick view on the external teams. The external teams are discussed in more detail in Chapter 6. The collective implementation project team is comprised of multiple sub team roles and responsibilities; the executive steering committee, the business process owners, the technology team, the core project team, the sustainment team, the stakeholder team and possibly other teams, depending upon your organization and culture. Let's discuss some of these different roles and responsibilities.

Your Internal Team

Champion

As part of the value assessment and business case effort, the executive champion(s), sometimes referred to as the sponsor(s), is identified. It may be obvious, but I will state it regardless, these champions should be as high up in the organization as possible. Ideally, the CEO should be brought in as the **champion** and if he/she will not have the time to be the **champion**, they should delegate to one of their able-bodied lieutenants who can keep the CEO updated. The logical candidate would be from a core business function and who has the "burning platform" issue etched into their skin. Also, the individual should come with a high level of respect in the organization to demonstrate company commitment to the implementation. The most successful sports franchises often have a very engaged owner driving a top down governance on the team and making sure the right skills, investments, tools, processes, coaching and chemistry are in place.

Executive Steering Committee

As you build the business case, keep the key contributors and stakeholders in mind. A number of these leaders should be the foundation of your **executive steering committee (ESC)**. The ones you will ultimately be accountable to serving and delivering. These should be the people that can remove enterprise obstacles and flatten major sticky organizational issues. These are also the people who will help sell the effort so that the business case gets approved. In many cases, the size of the investment may warrant reviewing the effort with your Board of Directors. The champion needs to be prepared for this and if the champion is not your CEO, your CEO obviously needs to be in synch prior to any Board review. Once approval is received for some or all aspects of the initiative, a project kickoff follows.

Coaching Moment - Accidental exclusion of the right executive(s) on your steering committee can lead to very negative consequences. A major transformation project costing hundreds of millions of dollars did not have the CFO on the ESC. The project neared global template rollout after completing pilots. Some global rollout re-planning was needed. The ESC was aligned with the program since they were on a regular monthly review with the program but the CFO was not and made the decision to not proceed with the program. This is an extreme example of poor executive governance and leadership but it demonstrates the critical nature of strong and effective governance on the program success and having the right leaders fully engaged.

The Stakeholder Team

This team is comprised of members and influencers not on the core team who should be engaged and made aware of the ERP project status. They are directly or indirectly impacted. The ESC consists of the most influential stakeholders but other stakeholders need to be managed through effective communications to get their feedback and avoid surprises. Stakeholders are key to setting the stage for the transformative change and responsible for helping to manage the change within their organization. Since there are so many different stakeholders and different roles, different approaches are obviously used to address them. It is common to maintain a list of stakeholders and assign them to members of the core team to cover to assure an adequate level of appropriate communications occur with them. Stakeholder management will be discussed more in Chapter 4. Note: ERP projects, even if your core finance processes are not in scope, require some level of Finance/Accounting team active participation in the program and sign off. Every ERP process ultimately seems to touch finance at some point. Make sure you have the finance team and their stakeholders actively on board throughout the design, realization, testing and go-live. The goal is to avoid getting to the first quarter close with the new solution and having finance escalate that nothing is working as it should be. Year end and quarter end closes often dictate go-live timing.

Program/Project Executive

The project executive is the client who leads the overall ERP or packaged application program initiative. This is a critical role. They are accountable for the project implementation. They should have experience with process transformation and packaged applications, be an effective communicator and ideally have some prior experience with ERP, since the complexity of ERP projects is unique. They will lead the program management office to provide overall governance to the program.

One of the organizational cultural challenges I have experienced at large corporations is the related selection process. The top leadership opts to put someone who is not familiar with their ERP and packaged applications in place to lead the team. Often times the client thinking is, this is an up and coming corporate leader so let them become instrumental in the ERP project so they learn our new way of doing business. It might work out OK if this leader then surrounds himself/herself with competent internal ERP savvy people but even that is a big risk. Ideally, the corporation will select a leader that will have the wounds of an ERP implementation on their resume, even if it means going outside to find someone. It doesn't mean the internal candidate is not a good leader without that ERP experience, it just means they are not the best candidate to lead the ERP project. ERP implementations are not like past IT efforts or projects. Their complexities are often unparalleled when compared to other transformation projects. Commercial consulting teams love to see client leaders without ERP and vendor management skills at the helm. Many times these consulting teams play the lack of ERP depth on the customer side for all it is worth, literally. On one project with a leader without any ERP experience, I saw consulting labor burn rates well in excess of $100M/year only to still not have the right resources to execute and fall woefully short of the goal line.

I have also seen situations where the client hired a proven outsider and ERP leader who had done successful ERP projects at other firms. This individual made a significant difference in the engagement. He asked the right questions, governed the packaged software supplier and the SI effectively and ultimately led the team to a successful project implementation that met the expectations of the business.

The obvious net here, the right skilled leadership is a critical element to success. You can win without the right leaders (coaches) as sometimes the team skills and efforts can overcome this, but it is always better to compete with the best team across the board.

The executive steering committee may delegate aspects of leadership to the project executive on the core project team but regardless, the buck stops with them. The ESC are often the ultimate decision makers accountable to the CEO and Board. They are the ones in charge of the investment in the initiative as well as the return on investment to the business, holding the process owners and business units responsible for delivering on the business case.

Program Management Office (PMO)

The PMO is usually led by the program/project executive and its members often include application supplier leadership, systems integrator leadership and the project manager. It is the main day to day governing body for the ERP or packaged application program and meets regularly to review the high-level status of the program. It provides program direction guidance and addresses inhibitors, risk management and issues and as needed, and prepares readouts for delivery by the program/project executive to the executive steering committee. It should govern the project scope, roadmap and plan and address scope change requests or enhancement requests that are significant. This governance includes the Best Practice of setting the direction for minimized packaged application customization.

Coaching Moment - Some PMOs don't do a good job of managing scope or packaged application customizations. This inability to minimize customization results in significant process complexity and both incremental additional development costs and the burden costs of carrying that customization into on-going yearly support costs. The degree of customization in an ERP project is a metric that should be visible with measurable value realization metrics assigned to respective process owners.

I participated in one PMO in a customer role and observed that the systems integrator had more members on the PMO team than the client representatives. I strongly advised the customer executive to increase the client representation. The customer

executive surprisingly not only dismissed the advice but actually reduced the client team membership on the governing body at the advice of the SI. Eventually this program derailed and one of the causes can be attributed to the overwhelming influence that the SI had on decision making. The customer leadership did not fully understand that the SI was there to make recommendations and the client team had to make the decisions, to not just accept every recommendation the SI made.

Business Process Owners

The business process owners (BPOs) are the identified owners of the processes being transformed. It is ideal if they are engaged in the key enterprise process blueprinting/exploration but if not, they should have delegates participating with the core project team. These BPOs are absolutely critical to the transformation desired. It is incumbent upon them to help coach and motivate their teams through the change. People do not like change in general and resistance will manifest itself in multiple ways. The BPOs must continually be an advocate for change and also put their money where their mouth is. This holds true of any of their delegates as well. "Super users", also known as "power users" or "key users", must come from the business and the BPOs are the ones who should identify and commit them to the program. BPOs are also intimately involved in the business case, value realization and benefit identification.

I have observed that an area lacking is the BPO for master data, as transformation of processes often has roots tied to effective management of master data. If customer master, material master, HR record master, vendor master, finance master and other key master data is lacking a clear end to end process ownership, valuable time will be lost and the initiative will spin. It could potentially spell delay or instability in go-live that will not be easily resolved without master data enterprise process ownership. If your organization can't easily identify the respective master data process owners during the very early planning phase of the project, the PMO or executive steering committee needs to address this major gap and staff the master data process owner role(s) with a top leader. I have been sharing stories and lessons learned about the critical nature of master data for a successful ERP project since SAP R/3 came on the scene in the early 1990's, and it is incredible the number of organizations that still don't have a formalized management of their enterprise master data process in place. You would not go into a regular season without being properly prepared or without all of the team roles staffed and still expect to win, e.g., starting pitchers, field goal kicker, forwards, point guard, so why do we find businesses jumping into packaged application implementations without thinking about clean master data and who owns that data. In Chapter 5, we spend more time discussing business processes and master data.

One additional point on business process owners. It is critical that BPOs be empowered to lead and make enterprise process changes to align with the packaged application off-the-self capabilities. If their title is lip service only or they are not capable of leading to drive the process change, this will be very detrimental to your packaged application transformation and your goal of winning. They also need to hold the line on change requests once the scope is locked down. Change requests can cripple an implementation and BPOs need to help limit the changes and not be the one piling them on.

Corporate Standards Teams

This topic is likely limited to larger global corporations with the needs to justify these teams. They usually have roles to architect process, data and technology and architecture boards and other teams that guide the enterprise in the use of standards. The goal being standardization for warranted areas of the business to avoid many one-offs that drive up costs but don't add value to the enterprise. A good example is a corporate technology team. The core project technology domain team, responsible for the technology being rolled out to support the ERP software package, e.g., the database, the infrastructure, the network, the security, should collaborate with members of the enterprise architecture and technology team to make sure the ERP rollout is not an island unto itself with one-of-a-kind technology that does not align with the enterprise architecture. The corporate standards and architecture team should be engaged in technology heavy ERP decisions to assure that technology stack issues do not creep up in the future or that any new technology being adopted is incorporated within the enterprise standards. For instance, if a middleware standard already exists across the corporation what is the impact of the ERP vendor middleware stack. If there is existing middleware in place in the company, will the packaged application vendor's middleware replace the existing standard or integrate with it?

The Core Project Team

This is the team that will plan and perform the day to day work required to develop and deploy the ERP project and template. This team is comprised of the respective process domains and process owners (or their delegates, as a second choice). Other domains include the development and technology domain, master data domains, compliance and controls domain, an organizational change management (OCM) domain and participation from the CoE sustainment domain. Each of the domains typically starts off with leads who represent the client, e.g., O2C domain lead, and are paired with the systems integrator lead for the given domain. This is often referred to as a "two in the box" model with the client domain leader teamed with an ERP package consulting leader. A note regarding the master data domain. Often, the master data domain is managed as a sub domain of the respective process domains. This can work but given the critical nature that master data plays in ERP projects, creating a domain specifically for master data is easily justified. Given the fact that most ERP projects which fail to meet expectations can be traced to problems with the "soft stuff", the organizational change domain is warranted in some form. If the OCM domain and focus does not exist, it is typically the result of executive thinking that believes these "soft stuff" items will be dealt with by the rest of the domain teams. If you look at a typical OCM domain, it is responsible for stakeholder management, communications, training and value realization tracking through the initial phases of the project and will transfer these ongoing responsibilities to the sustainment team (CoE) once live. Therefore, if you do not have the OCM domain, then those responsibilities still need to be managed explicitly.

The people selected from the business to participate in the core project team should be the 'A' team for each respective team, whether it is finance, order to cash, procure to pay, HR, or any other process or business unit. These should be your best people with the reputation for getting things done the right way and not taking "no" for an answer. These should be the people that you can least afford to pull from their assignments. There may be some hesitation from the business units to provide their "A" team members to be a part of the core team for a variety of reasons, e.g., overstretch already stretched people, offering their best people for an extended period of time will negatively impact their results, ... This resistance is understandable but must not be accepted since any team looking to win always puts their best players on the field. Governance should make sure this doesn't happen.

Coaching Moment: Your internal team members should be full-time on the ERP project. Part-time participants don't have the commitment necessary to get things done. Don't spend millions of dollars on consultants and refuse to backfill a $75,000/year role. Note: the smaller the company the more difficult it is to achieve this full-time commitment so be fully cognizant of it. Plan and prepare for a workable approach and actively monitor it and adjust as needed.

Another point on the core team on larger projects, it is typically augmented by a local sub-team that is established. Local teams are important as part of the extended team to help address country/region specific process and technology needs and augment the core organizational change management team with local change management skills to facilitate the business adoption of the solution in the region.

If your solution is hosted on-premise, your infrastructure team likely will be internal and part of the core team. However, you may opt for outsourcing your on-premise infrastructure or leverage a cloud hosted solution and use an external team. Your core internal team should still have a role responsible for managing that external infrastructure relationship.

Project management for the core team may be provided by your SI, you or some combination. A collaborative project effort is required between the SI, application vendor and your team to work as one. There needs to be good team chemistry here as well as governance oversight to achieve effective delivery and avoid finger pointing. If there is a lot of friction and animosity, especially as things get difficult, program governance needs to intervene and take the necessary steps to remedy it. I have seen SI project managers released from the project because they do not get along well with other team members. You will succeed as a team or fail as a team.

Project tracking and status updates are part of the regular project team cadence. Full transparency and accountability need to be in place and information should not be hidden away in some secret spreadsheet. Realtime dashboards of meaningful project key performance indicators (KPIs) should be available to the project team to view the status and project health. Managing or governing the wrong things ends in poor results. For example, one project executive focused maniacally on tracking customizations only to end up with an enormous amount of customization due to poor governance, drowning the project.

The sustainment team is a vital team to establish and the sooner the better. I will often use the Center of Excellence (CoE) term interchangeably with the Sustainment team. Within this book and much of the industry, they are referred to as one in the same. A Best Practice seen within the industry is identifying a CoE leader upfront to participate in the project planning and kickoff or even beforehand with the Value Assessment and Business Case development. Being involved with the details of how a solution is developed and built makes the transition to sustaining it a much smoother effort.

The CoE team is usually the "last man standing" as the Core project team completes development and initial rollouts. As the Systems Integrator team members and their respective expertise transition off the project, typically client SMEs within the Core team are planned to transition into the CoE, as these Core team members have the solution knowledge. A "cross-walk" exercise, meaning analyzing core team members and determining which should be boarded into the CoE should be thought out before go-live and executed as the solution stabilizes, the core team ramps down and the CoE ramps up. Also, as the core OCM domain team ramps down, its mission of communications, stakeholder management, training and most importantly value realization tracking, are transitioned into the CoE with appropriate staffing levels. Value realization (VR) is such an important business topic yet many ERP projects that are live in the sustainment phase do not have any single VR focal point which often results in the business lacking someone who is responsible for tracking and measuring against the initial business case commitments.

"Super users"/"key users" need to be highlighted on your checklist if you are to realize the value of your packaged application implementation. I have a preference for the "Super" adjective for these users, though they are also called key users, power users… "Super" reminds me of Superman or Superwoman and the superpowers they will need in order to help transform the culture. These are your best employees in each respective process area who will be wed to the project from initiation through keeping the solution humming when it is operational. They play so many crucial roles. They must possess the ability to transition into being subject matter experts (SMEs) of the application and solution to help fill the void in package knowledge expertise when your external consultants exit after go-live. These super user roles are crucial to getting even greater value realization from your investment and helping to drive user adoption of the solution.

End users are the users of the packaged application solution being implemented. They can be from your internal organization, or from external organizations, like suppliers or customers. Super users are drawn from the end user community. Driving end user business adoption of the solution is key to business success and discussed in detail in Chapter 4.

External Team Members

The **packaged application software supplier** is obviously a critical partner. They provide the software package, package consulting, support expertise, sales and account management, and top to top relationship commitment. Chapter 6, Technology, contains much more detail on the packaged application supplier, the engagement model, roles and lessons learned and Best Practices.

The **systems integrator (SI) team** is another critical cog in your implementation and support of the packaged application. The classic expensive Big Four consulting houses come to mind immediately with their army of consultants but there are also many local boutique firms that can do the job or provide MVP type players on a more as-needed basis. The SI consultants are brought on board to help you augment your team skills with deep experienced application and technical know-how. Keeping track of all of these skills is a vital aspect for value realization. Ultimately, a goal is to transition the SI team expertise to your in-house team. So it is not only vital to keep track of the SI team burn rate and skills being provided but also to make sure that there is a clearly defined and executable knowledge transfer process in place to ramp up the skills of your super users to become self-sufficient. More detail on the systems integrator, the engagement model, roles, lessons learned and Best Practices are covered in Chapter 6, Technology.

Special advisory roles are team members who bring very unique ERP package implementation skills to the team. Think of them as the specialized advisor that you bring in for a specific challenge or issue. These advisory consultants that you hire to coach your team through the topic can come from the packaged application vendor, a systems integrator or independent consultants. All options offer a different set of skills, degree of vendor independence and costs, to address the complex software, technology, project delivery and governance issues that arise. Obviously, the independent consultant, in addition to their skills and expertise, brings an objective and independent outside view. I have seen customers bring in an independent consultant for an assessment of the overall program/project at key junction points to share recommendations. This provided immense value to the customers. This includes invaluable independent feedback on the SI team. I discuss the independent advisory consulting role more in Chapter 6.

Sports teams select advisors who have played the game or been involved with it for a long time. They have demonstrated skills that line up with organizational culture. The best advisors and coaches build a culture of motivation, innovation, optimism and teamwork that translates into winning programs year over year.

Note that there are over 70 different ERP packages available, e.g., SAP, Oracle, Infor, Microsoft, and a similarly high number of offerings exist for other packaged applications areas like CRM, HCM and ITSM. These packages have varying degrees of capabilities and integration. If you are in the early stages of package selection, it is wise to draw on an experienced advisory consultant to help augment and coach you and your team through the selection process on an as-needed basis. There are seasoned veterans in the ERP and packaged application space with 30 or more years of experiences that can be invaluable to your success.

Figure 2 provides an example of an ERP/packaged application project team structure and roles. This is just an example and depending upon a number of factors, e.g., scope, size, geography, the structure may be adjusted. In a small to mid-size company, these roles/responsibilities likely translate into the wearing of multiple hats by the same team members. For example, the project executive may effectively be the PMO, the change management lead and a process owner. Each of the team roles discussed earlier has critical responsibilities that should be addressed. How and by whom depends but your plan needs to acknowledge and reflect it.

Team Structure – Role/Responsibility Example

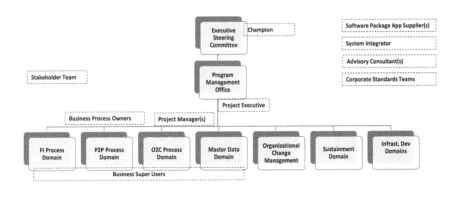

Copyright, STX Consulting

Figure 2- Team Structure – Role/Responsibility Example

The Team and Governance

Governance, as a key ingredient in winning the game, is worth noting here and it is exercised on multiple levels of the team. From project managers, to program/project executive and the PMO up through the executive steering committee and ultimately the Board of Directors, effective proactive governance should be applied. The PMO, with its program executive, should be the main governing project body as they are the direct link to the steering committee, and the program executive will provide the readout to the Board. Chapter 4, People/Culture, will describe in detail many lessons learned and governance OCM Best Practices related to the team roles and responsibilities.

More detail on governance for the external teams, the application suppliers(s) and the systems integrator, is covered in Chapter 6. Note that the application suppliers(s) plural indicates that your packaged application project can possibly require more than one packaged application supplier. A number of larger ERP projects often have bolt-on applications for the ERP application package that provide unique customer needed functions, e.g., tax calculations, sales price margin management, transportation optimizations .... So even though the ERP package has a much larger footprint, it is important to govern these bolt-ons within the same governing model.

Let's next discuss some additional background on packaged application efforts that will facilitate our transition to more detail and coaching insight on the pillars of transformation.

Chapter 3 – The Essentials of Packaged Application Transformation

"What's dangerous is not to evolve, not to invent, not to improve the customer experience."
Jeff Bezos, Amazon Founder

People/Culture, Business Processes and Technology

By default, implementation of a packaged application drives the business to undergo transformation and evolve from doing what you do today to doing it differently, more efficiently, with greater agility to improve your customers' experience. The packaged applications have a set of (configurable) **Business Processes** that are enabled during the implementation as well as roles and responsibilities for your **People** that are required to execute those processes. The underlying **Technology** of the packaged application is comprised of the software package, the software supplier and systems integrator technology expertise melded with your team's business expertise and the hardware infrastructure (on-premise or in the cloud).

The essentials to your business transformation are:

People – Who are the users and being impacted?
Process – How do we do the work (tasks and structure)?
Technology – What tools do we use to do the work?

In order to enable the underlying packaged application project to establish the new processes, roles and responsibilities, you team with the packaged application software supplier and needed consulting expertise to augment your internal team. You leverage the packaged application supplier's methodology to develop a plan and execute the plan. First, to implement the new processes and second, to operate, enhance and maintain the new processes to satisfy your customer's needs.

The Project Plan

The project plan for your project implementation is critical. There are many unique consulting methodologies. However, all are based on the underlying application supplier methodology. Some methodology examples are SAP ASAP methodology and the new Activate methodology, Oracle AIM methodology, Infor Deployment Method and Microsoft Dynamics Sure Step Methodology.

Develop a plan that is realistic, addressing business alignment and organizational change and has a timeframe that does not exhaust the patience of an organization, e.g., bring a plan forward that provides at a minimum a reasonable go-live time with some tangible benefits. As mentioned earlier, small and mid-size companies will have fewer individuals on the team taking on multiple roles and critical responsibilities.

Implementation phases with exit criteria, should not be viewed as optional. This seems like such an obvious item that it is hard to believe the number of project plans that get drawn up without documented criteria serving as a gate before proceeding. Placing criteria in place that should be satisfied before allowing the project to exit one phase before advancing to the next are a Best Practice. A scenario that I see pop up is having the exit criteria defined but relaxing the governance rules to allow the initiative to move forward without thoroughly understanding the root causes of why the criteria were not met. Having exit criteria (or phase entry criteria) help assure that the right levels of analysis, testing and rigor have been exercised before allowing the team to shift its focus. Strong governance can effectively define the criteria up front, communicate it clearly and then monitor the project and team in meeting these. Note: I am aware of instances where "the date is the date" and the program must go live, e.g., a divestiture and contractual commitments. There is no "pause button" option. Up front planning becomes even more critical as does mitigation planning and proactive governance. Good headlights are needed into issues with strong communications needed across the organization.

Cloud based solutions, among other things, amplify the need for establishing a core internal OCM capability. Once again, in smaller and mid-size companies this might be through wearing multiple hats and/or some level of staff augmentation. Cloud solutions accelerate the pace of transformation and business change. Application vendors roll out new function into their cloud offerings at an accelerated pace for your business to adapt, especially when compared to the on-premise model. Communications, stakeholder management and training all need to be aligned with the increased rate of business change. Not to mention areas outside of OCM such as more responsive testing demands with the increased rate of application features by the supplier as well as organizational structure impact to your CoE sustainment team with the changing solution support needs.

Implement, Rollout and Sustain

It is important to note two distinct workstreams to the packaged application program. The first workstream is to implement the design and rollout/deployment across the identified geographies in scope. The concept of a global template is a Best Practice for global rollouts. The global template establishes the elements of the global design which are built, and localizations are added to the template as needed for each respective region. The core project team is assisted by the local extended teams in the regional/local rollouts. While the solution template is being rolled out at different timepoints to different geographies, each go-live leaves a live operating solution that the business in that region is using to run its day to day business. That solution needs to be supported and sustained. This is the second workstream, the sustainment of the solution while the core team continues on with the global rollout. In order to free up the core team from maintaining a recently deployed solution, the CoE takes over the reins of sustaining the solution via a transition that happens during the hypercare phase of the project immediately after go-live. The hypercare support phase during go-live is discussed more later in the book.

Depending on the size and scope (on-premise vs cloud, only one geography, your organization,....) of your packaged application project, will determine how large and the structure of your core project team and CoE sustainment team as well as the dynamics around the deployments and support. Key roles and responsibilities may be covered by the same person but responsibility mapping should still be addressed. This is usually part of the planning discussion as "rollout roadmaps" are updated from the high-level business case views.

Scope and Change Request Management

These are critical success factors. In order to make the plan achievable it is vital to limit any scope change requests to mission critical changes approved by the ESC, e.g., a new divestiture or acquisition needs to be addressed within the plan. Any customization or modifications required to satisfy needed business capabilities that are identified as gaps in the standard package capability must be scrutinized and judiciously assessed with strong governance before inclusion in the solution. A change control board needs to be put in place and should get accustomed to saying "No" or "deferred" to change requests. In a small to mid-size company, the project executive may have the luxury to mandate use of the out-of-the-box package. Clear communications on the change request governance policy should be shared across all business stakeholders and teams. A business rule that I have seen be particularly effective at limiting change requests on larger projects is to require the requesting organization to fund (tax) not only the initial effort but any annual incremental support costs that arise from the change.

An acronym associated with customization in the SAP world is the term WRICEF. It implies development required for Workflows, Reports, Interfaces, Conversions, Enhancements (via supplier provided software hooks) and Forms (WRICEF). You need to govern the WRICEF requirement related discussions and in general, limit this to the essential. The fewer the WRICEFs the lower your cost of implementation and on-going support. This customization discussion is relevant for any packaged application. Going outside the realm of enhancements where you don't use the supplier package hooks and your team creates code modifications is a very poor practice. Ideally, the business requirements that drive this type of packaged application modification request should be identified early and used as a priority in the software supplier selection process. If no software supplier can meet the requirement without modifying their software, you can find out how those types of requirements are addressed in the industry and use that input as an option to consider.

Coaching Moment – Be careful in quickly, unobjectively coming to the conclusion that there is no value in understanding the legacy as-is processes. Many companies come to this conclusion for the wrong reasons – "it would be too difficult and costly to understand how we do what we do today and/or we are going to use out-of-the-box ERP so just ignore it." The approach of mandating out-of-the-box may be viable at a small to mid-size company where the culture and governance supports this adoption. However, a valuable exercise is meeting with stakeholders and super users up front in understanding key steps in the as-is processes and identifying items that may cause future real gaps. The lack of clarity on how processes run in the as-is view can be a major contributing factor to last minute design change requests or unclear requirements already in the scope. Also, having the up-front key requirements conversations with stakeholders and super users will strengthen those communications channels for future dialogue.

Analytical process mining tools are now readily available to quickly and affordably uncover the as-is process view with full objective process transparency. This can help avoid the project feedback that "we didn't really understand the as-is process when we first discussed it" or "we thought the out-of-the-box capabilities would address this". If you do the process mining analysis early in the prep/design phase, you have the as-is process facts and are able to identify where the customer value-add steps are. This enables having a fact-based logical discussion of what the business needs are versus what the business wants. Process mining enables an objective fact-based analysis on the to-be processes also. More information on process mining tools later.

Project Change Control Board (CCB)

A key aspect of any project is dealing with scope change requests. These can come from the business in response to business needs, legal or regulatory requirements or technical needs such as applying software supplier patches. The project change control board can be comprised of several leaders from the team for a larger team or merely the project executive for a small to mid-sized team. The CCB plays the vital role to review and approve/deny submitted changes. The CCB membership skills need to be able to synthesize data being provided to quantify and qualify the request to make a decision on how to disposition the change request. Ideally, the membership includes senior leadership with a solid understanding of the business and an aptitude for technical insight to distill the input provided by the change request sponsor into a yes/no decision on the request. Remember, approving change requests have been known to sink a program as costs and time of developing and delivering the solution increase. Additionally, the often not addressed issue of burdened long-term support cost is overlooked in the decision-making process only to raise its head in the future with the business overwhelmed at the costs to support the solution. It is an often overlooked "kick the can down the road" story.

Common Challenges to Any Transformation

Some people may initially believe this to be a simple and straight forward project, but ERP applications have caused more than their fair share of disappointment. Remember the introductory statement that over 70% of these projects don't meet expectations. Even if it is half of that number, that is a large percentage of very costly projects that are not meeting expectations. These are difficult projects.

There are many major challenges to business transformation:

People – changing mindsets and corporate culture, lack of change management knowledge, lack of executive management commitment, the wrong program leadership, resource shortages, not committing to your super user community

Process – complexity is not understood and/or underestimated, changes to processes, lack of process ownership, master data issues

Technology – selecting the wrong partners, not planning for a sustainment team, no transition plans

The keys to successful transformation are based on proactively addressing challenges within your plans with active governance. The next three chapters (Chapter 4 – People/Culture, Chapter 5 – Processes and Master Data and Chapter 6 – Technology) address the challenges shared above and more. Many of these key challenges point to the need to establish, at a very early stage of the project, an organizational change management (OCM) component role and responsibility within the organization. If you do not already have an OCM team within your organization, a Best Practice is to establish an OCM responsibility in parallel with your packaged application implementation. You should identify a candidate to lead this element and have them work "two in the box" with the SI Consulting organizational change management leader from the early project preparation phases through the cycle to go live. This internal person should be targeted to ultimately join your CoE sustainment team. This makes perfect sense since your CoE team will likely be assuming the change management on-going responsibilities of communications, training, stakeholder management. It always worries me when I see a lack of commitment (funding) by the business to some level of OCM representation from the business in the project and even worse, after post go-live. Given the overwhelming evidence of the critical nature OCM plays in the successful implementation and successful value realization after go-live, it needs to be a priority. I have seen business leaders defer to the consulting OCM lead with the notion that OCM is some effort that is time-boxed with the project implementation. Once the project goes live, there is no longer a need for OCM. The result without OCM input is the project may go live but the value realization will fall flat as continued business adoption is not managed.

Coaching Moment: A Best Practice is to establish an internal organizational change management responsibility in the preparation phase and since this role should persist after go live, it makes a lot of sense to align the role with the Center of Excellence (CoE) which will provide solution sustainment support. This internal OCM role can team with your SI change management lead as part of the knowledge transfer and transition planning process. More about the CoE and transition process later as these are vital to success and value realization.

Avoiding the "Red Team" Review and a Troubled Project

When a "Red Team" review is needed, that is usually not good news. It means your project has significant challenges that need to be addressed. ("Red" signaling an urgent situation). I have been called in to help stabilize troubled packaged application projects many times. This includes what I refer to as the "Red Adair" scenario. (Coincidentally also named "Red", Red Adair became famous for being called in to fight out-of-control oil and gas well blowout wildfires.) In one situation, the customer who had called me in was losing customers and millions of dollars of revenue every week after a troubled go-live. They were barely able to ship product and when they were able to ship product it was uncertain if the delivery was correct. Their processes were broken. This was an out-of-control scenario of a company going live with their ERP project when they should not have.

I have also been called in as a reviewer as part of a "Red Team" to do an assessment prior to go live to try to put the project back on course when major design challenges were everywhere, from bad and incomplete customer data loads to performance issues that threatened any attempt at cutting over to go-live. During these review sessions it is not unusual to collaborate with the packaged application supplier's key troubleshooting resources, to remedy major issues that have been identified and are gating the project from proceeding.

"Red Team" reviews mean dire straits. How do you avoid and mitigate these situations? Proactive governance around the organizational change, business processes, master data and technology can be the solution. In the first red team example above with the out-of-control go-live, there were a litany of red flags prior to go-live that backed up into the early stages of the project plan that phase exit and entry criteria should have mitigated if governed properly and in the second situation, better design oversight and governance with earlier qualification of design gaps would have mitigated it. Even if the "cat is already out of the bag", establishing enhanced proactive governance can improve your coaching, program direction and results. Proactive governance is about gaining the insight and visibility to get ahead of issues before they turn into major issues. By "skating to where the puck is going to be, not where it has been," as Wayne Gretzky said, you will put yourself in a better position to play the game.

In the chapters that follow, I will share more insight into how to develop a better proactive governance model, starting with the people and culture.

Chapter 4 – Getting Your Team into "The Zone" - People/Culture

"One thing I know for sure is that we all have a trigger that puts us in the zone. Something that ignites our competitive intensity, laser focus and a relentless craving to attack and conquer."

Tim S. Grover – Personal trainer for an esteemed group of former and current NBA Players including Michael Jordan.

Organizational change management (OCM) is required to get your people, culture and business team aligned around the new packaged application transformation project to assure successful business adoption. Clayton Christensen, a Harvard Business School professor known for his theory of disruptive innovation, was spot on in noting that it is profoundly difficult for traditional companies to change. There is rarely a larger business transformation project than an ERP initiative and it will run head on into the realization that change management and the people component are front and center. If you treat the project as a technical endeavor it will fail. ERP involves people and business change. You have heard the term in sports when a team is on a roll and it seems like the ball is always bouncing their way while they dominant the game. It is commonly referred to as being in "the zone". I will share some of the key challenges faced in getting ERP teams fully aligned with the business and each other and insight, guidance and Best Practices to get your team into "the zone" to play at the intensity level required in order to win.

In Chapter 2 we introduced the internal and external teams and individuals involved in the project. In this chapter, we will focus on the project change management and the change leaders. The project team leadership and change management team, the stakeholders and the super users are all key project change leaders. The super users and stakeholders will receive special attention in this chapter because of their critical nature to the business acceptance and adoption of the solution during the implementation as well as the on-going operation and value realization activities for the project.

There are a number of industry change management models that focus on OCM impact, including PROSCI's ADKAR (Awareness, Desire, Knowledge, Ability and Reinforcement) and Kotter's "8 Step Process for Leading Change (now Accelerate Change)" models. While each has its own approaches, these all address the human side of change in organizational contexts. We build on those principles here.

Organizational change management helps to ensure that the new processes resulting from a packaged application transformation project are *actually* adopted by the people who are affected. Organizational change focuses on enabling a systemic shift in organizational behavior and culture. It concentrates on such intangibles as leadership, alignment, commitment, direction, expectations, and messaging. Many of these are longer term efforts outside the bounds of the ERP project and some people refer to this as the "soft stuff" on an ERP or packaged application project. Their purpose is to make sure everyone in the organization is on the same page and is going in the same direction. Additionally, and more specifically, to the new processes your new packaged software will introduce, change management must include identifying the specific tasks by department, role, and person necessary for your organization to execute your new processes successfully.

Change management reduces the risk that a new system or other change will be rejected by the enterprise. By itself OCM does not increase sales or reduce costs. Instead, it helps to build and increase the teamwork required by the business to accept the change and operate more efficiently.

Large ERP OCM teams may consist of a dozen or more people. A small organization in which the business changes will impact a smaller number of end users might ask a single individual to take on driving the OCM effort. Indeed, the OCM effort in smaller businesses may not even have its own dedicated people; rather, it might take up a percentage of a team member's time. For example, the project manager might be charged with handling it and/or spread across the project's process team(s), each team owning the management of change for its respective organization and end users.

With large packaged application efforts, demands from business process changes, interfaces to other systems, data cleanup and a number of other significant tasks, the need for dedicated OCM resources arise. If the OCM effort is not started concurrently with the rest of the program, it may only be started when the program team experiences resistance from end users who feel neglected and suspect. Reeling in that resistance is more difficult the later you get OCM involved in the program, so start early.

Some organizations, even today after all that has been written and shared about how critical it is to the project success, give OCM lip service. Even enterprises that assert that OCM is critical sometimes reduce or eliminate the OCM budget if the overall program runs into budgetary problems. I saw one very large project leadership team decide to reduce OCM staffing and move the related responsibility to an already burdened CoE team with no incremental resources or funding. The leadership treated OCM as some ancillary nice to have activity. The OCM component suffered significantly.

Coaching Moment – Don't cut corners with your OCM efforts or else be prepared for major post go-live issues or even pre go-live issues. It is certainly a pay me now or pay me a lot more later situation. Eventually you will pay and the "later" scenario is almost always significantly more costly and harder to fix. Take the OCM needs seriously and confirm it is in the plan and is getting done.

Major Steps in Addressing People/Culture Change

The OCM program has to adapt and change dynamically to accommodate the vagaries of human nature as supporters backslide and skeptics become supporters.

For companies of all sizes, the scope of an OCM effort is usually similar:

- Get the business ready.
- Prepare the people.
- Manage the transition.

There are different approaches to addressing this OCM scope, but most package implementation major steps address this scope in detail and can be summarized as follows:

1. Change Readiness and Communications Preparation. The program begins when the champion starts looking to transform the business. Ideally, a value assessment and business case are developed up front to drive alignment with the corporate strategic goals. As part of this activity, the champion helps to create a high-level vision describing how the enterprise will operate after the change has been implemented. This vision should include the high-level benefits that will accrue to the enterprise and should describe how the change will affect people. Ideally, improvements to the work environment will be obvious to the majority of the business and system users.

The OCM team identifies all departments, business units and groups that will need to change along with key stakeholders in each. In parallel, the OCM team analyzes how the various parts of the change will impact the way that people perform their jobs (RACI chart - (Responsible, Accountable, Consulted, Informed)). This analysis enables the OCM team to answer the most common question posed during a major change, "How does this impact me?"

As part of engagement, the OCM team discusses the coming change with potential supporters and stakeholders to determine their willingness to support the change and to create a sense of urgency across the business to implement the change. Identified stakeholders should be eager to support the change and share insight, risks and issues. The OCM team uses this and other input to identify likely skeptics and attempts to determine their concerns. In many cases, the team may draft a change readiness assessment to gain a more precise understanding of the enterprise's willingness to change.

As it becomes more obvious via interviews and discussions which stakeholders support the change, which are undecided, and which don't support the change, the OCM team creates a change plan with specific actions for each individual and group. Individual OCM members are assigned to work with individual stakeholders based in part on the strength of the relationship between the OCM team member and the specific stakeholder. Stakeholder management and analysis is a key OCM workstream throughout the project. Stakeholders should be included from all the different business units that are affected by the ERP implementation. They need to be part of the matrixed buy-in plan and part of the business case justification for the project. These are the people that will experience the process changes the greatest, so they need to be a major element of your organizational change management plan as well as wired into the user acceptance process. This includes business unit membership on the super user team. If the business unit users don't like what they're getting, they won't use it, or they will not use it effectively, and your value realization will suffer dramatically. Stakeholders will have to live with the system long after it's been implemented so bring them into the conversation from the start. Their nominated super users should keep them well informed of the user perspective.

Coaching Moment - The complexity of change management within the project isn't always well understood, well communicated, or dealt with. A comprehensive OCM plan is needed up front. Engaging with and managing stakeholders from the start is invaluable to getting a sense of issues and developing strong communications across the business. Working with the business stakeholders to capture the nuances and key steps within the as-is processes will aid the to-be design significantly. I have found that getting stakeholders engaged early and checking with them often provides invaluable project input to understanding the organizational culture and dynamics.

2.Project Kickoff Messaging, Implementation and Rollout. During implementation, the OCM team communicates continually with individuals at all levels in the enterprise to gain their support for the change. Communications are another key workstream of the OCM team. Communications typically begin with a formal announcement from the CEO, ideally, or other senior executive, supported by a regular cadence of town hall meetings, videos, emails, login announcements, posters, etc. The OCM team hopes to empower supporters and help individuals or groups become successful quickly.

The OCM group identifies and celebrates successes publicly and rewards individuals responsible for each success.

As the rollout continues, surveys and/or interviews are used to better gauge employee acceptance and commitment to the change. For individuals and groups that appear reluctant to accept the change, resistance management techniques, discussed later, should be applied.

There are many key activities that occur during the implementation that are essential to addressing the needed change. Listed below are some key activities. Later in this chapter, we will map these activities to phases and workstreams supporting the implementation and operation to provide a clearer roadmap.

Training and Knowledge Transfer - Knowledge transfer and training are an on-going effort with different audiences throughout the project. The overall training plan is a critical change management ingredient. Infrastructure, data and solution readiness, are key dependencies in delivering the training. To quote Henry Ford on the training topic, *"The only thing worse than training your employees and having them leave is not training them and having them stay."*

New and Old Processes and Job Roles - To-be processes will introduce new roles and responsibilities and likely eliminate some old processes and corresponding roles and responsibilities. It is critical to address both the new roles and responsibilities and the disappearing roles and impact on the people in those roles. Will these people be utilized and trained for new roles or will they be without a new role and job? A plan will have to be developed by the OCM team working with the process owners, program leadership and HR, as needed, to address this. The new role planning is a standard part of an ERP engagement. As part of the to-be process activity a RACI chart is typically created for associated to-be roles and responsibilities. The mapping of people to roles is a key task that also serves as input into the segregation of duties (SoD) analysis as well as the security and authorization for role setup in the system. Additionally, process owners or other key stakeholders may need to be engaged to address budgetary funding needs for new roles within the organization.

Testing - Provides an excellent opportunity for the business super users to fully understand the solution and gain further and deeper knowledge in the to-be processes and provide feedback on the new processes before these processes are live.

3. Count Down to Go-Live and Transition to Running the Business. As go-live approaches, organizational change readiness checks should be an element of the overall project readiness for go-live. Knowledge transfer, training, super user preparedness, processes for boarding new team members and dealing with attrition, are examples of measurable criteria that need to be a part of the organization change readiness assessment.

Because people rarely behave as others would like them to behave, the OCM team regularly revisits and updates change goals, rewards, communications and consequences. Experience is the best teacher. Repeated interactions with individual stakeholders and super users usually reveal their degree of acceptance, enabling the OCM team to adjust the approach as necessary.

Individual performance plans should be updated to reflect tasks, projects and behaviors that support the changes needed by the project. Items in the performance plan need to be clear, measurable and achievable. In addition, these items need to be weighted appropriately against the other goals in the individual plans.

Change management is rarely straightforward though it may be depicted that way in the project plan. In practice, OCM activities rarely have clear tasks, precedents and durations. Most OCM teams cycle through the steps above multiple times during any OCM effort. Lessons learned at any point are incorporated into the OCM vision and communications. In many ways, the OCM work is never fully complete, much like continuous improvement plans (CIP). Change is constant in business. After go-live, the OCM mission should transfer to the CoE to carry forward in collaboration with the business.

Challenges - Why do Individuals Resist Change?

Resistance is a natural part of the change process. When expectations are disrupted, individuals often feel uncomfortable. Even positive changes such as a marriage, a new home or a new and better job, can cause stress and discomfort. Each individual exposed to a change goes through a process of evaluating and responding to the change. I am sure you have seen some version of the chart below of the phases of change people go through with a new project on the way to becoming enlightened and fully engaged and committed.

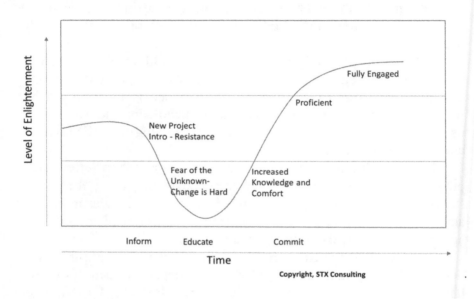

Figure 3 - Change Enlightenment Curve

Note there are many vagaries of human nature that are not depicted in the figure such as supporters backsliding while skeptics become supporters and move up the curve. Change dynamics within your organization need to be identified and managed. A discussion of a number of those dynamics follows.

Here are reasons why employees resist change and how it affects the change management process:

Inability. Individuals may lack the necessary skills or knowledge to operate in the new environment. Fear of the unknown can keep people from fully participating in training. Some worry they will not be able to understand how to operate the new system or will be overshadowed by smarter colleagues. Some groups may lack the resources to operate in the changed environment. This can be an issue when new processes require increased responsibilities and roles or when acquisitions occur. Acquisitions are often justified by claiming the merged companies will generate synergies by eliminating redundant jobs. Management is sometimes tempted to eliminate staff before the merger is fully complete and people are up to speed. Actions that result in inadequate resource levels to run a process typically disappoint customers, fragment staff loyalty, and erode IT service levels.

Unwillingness. People who don't believe in the change usually resist the change. Reasons vary but can include: They see no value to the new way of operating; they believe the change is too difficult; they perceive the change as too risky. Other people may believe the wrong option was selected. Still others worry their job will be less important and they will no longer be experts.

Let me share an example. Managing resistance from business managers who are heavily vested in continuing existing work practices and processes can be daunting. On a major transformation project, the CoE manager was chartered by the project executive with instituting the Best Practice of establishing super users as a first line of support for the business teams. The CoE manager ran into a peer business manager who was a well-connected long-time employee and whose whole team had effectively become an ad hoc support team for the legacy order to cash business process. That manager felt very threatened that his value-add and the value-add of his team would be undermined and they would be displaced or minimized, and certainly his role would diminish. The CoE manager tried to work with this business manager to develop a new workable model leveraging him and his team and continually communicating with him on the merits of the super user model as a proven Best Practice. This manager ended up being the worst kind of resistor. He indicated to the CoE manager that he was open to working on viable super user support models going forward while working behind the scenes with his network of other long time business managers and the executive program leaders to try and undermine the Best Practice super user support model and introduce doubt and why it would never work for their business due to the business process complexity. A huge amount of time was wasted on this resistor because he was the worst kind of resistor with his toxic behavior infecting his network of management buddies and undermining project efforts. The OCM team should have been more attuned, engaged and vocal on the issue. The program leadership and their governance responsibility should have put an immediate stop to this resistance and declared that super users were a key component of success going forward but instead they took a more passive stance, mildly stating the desire to go the route of the new super user based support model and not wanting to get some peer executive VP upset with the issue. This issue lingered for a long time after go-live causing a lack of commitment to the to-be super user support model, confusion and a negative impact on the overall success of the program.

Fatigue from Change. Change requires a great deal of mental effort. Whether it is the everyday life changes like buying a house, changing jobs or traveling abroad, these changes can introduce high levels of stress and mental change fatigue. Too many new systems, reorganizations, mergers, or other changes can also create change fatigue. After a time, most people crave stability; at some point few people will make the extra effort required to undertake one more change. Instilling a business culture of constant change and the ability to adapt and embrace it is not easy but a requirement for successful companies.

Personal issues. Few people lead perfect lives and most worry about something. Individuals close to retirement, facing divorce, serious illness, or other personal issues, frequently resist all changes in order to feel they retain some control over their life. Intellectually, these individuals may understand the reasons for the change but emotionally they often find it difficult or impossible to embrace the change. Handling each special case with compassion builds support for the change while insensitive handling can turn the rest of the enterprise against the change.

Resistance Management Techniques

Resistance is not necessarily a sign of disloyalty or incompetence. Usually, it shows that the resisting individuals either don't agree with the vision or lack the ability to implement the change. The best change management programs encourage people to discuss their concerns and never suppress dissent. After all, issues cannot be addressed if the OCM team does not know they exist.

Here are a few proven methods to address individual and group resistance:

- Educate and Communicate

- Leverage HR teams and Managers

- Leverage Stakeholders

- Leverage the Executive Team

- Acknowledge Real Issues and Risks and manage them

Coaching Moment – The OCM team and the program leadership need to be constantly aware of resistance and proactively manage it effectively and not let it fester and potentially become toxic to the program. The need for strong governance in support of the OCM effort when it comes to dealing with resistance is a critical success factor.

Cultural Norms are different around the globe. The OCM effort needs to be aware of local customs. When a change project spans multiple geographies and cultures, we must adapt our approach, even with a global system intended to standardize enterprise operations. Too often, global organizations disregard cultural nuances and fail to understand that the perception of change, organizational or otherwise, is not consistent across the world. Here are a few cultural factors that might impact your project and require adjusting your approach.

Communications style. Denmark, Germany, Israel, U.S. and Netherlands are very direct in communicating. India, Japan and the Philippines tend to be indirect and believe it is very important for both parties to save face. In these cultures, individuals avoid saying no, and frequently mean, "I understand" rather than "I agree" when they say "yes."

Sharing Authority. Cultures share power differently. Some place all authority and decision-making at the top of the organization, while others distribute the power more evenly. For example, in China, I have seen projects where nothing got done unless the executive at the top says it gets done. This was effectively the project management and project governance model. This doesn't mean that workers had no viewpoint or that they don't want to be consulted. It only meant that no action is taken unless it came from the top.

Time orientation. Meetings in Germany, Switzerland, and the U.S. start and end when scheduled (usually). Little time is dedicated to introductions, even when some attendees are meeting each other for the first time. Spain, Thailand and Brazil are less concerned about time. Things can wait. In such countries it is impolite to rush into a business discussion; only after the host and the visitor have shared refreshments and pleasantries should business begin.

The best OCM teams are very sensitive to local cultural norms even when the executive push is for a standard project rollout and standard OCM program globally. The OCM team needs to coach, communicate and advise to pre-empt these issues. As a Best Practice, global initiatives should have OCM extended teams with members from the regions to help address the local needs and norms.

Millennials and Generational Dynamics

It is worth noting some unique generational dynamics across your team members. Millennials (Generation Y or Gen Y) have joined the workforce and are now likely to be a key part of your organization and team. The shifting demographics of the workforce where millennials will comprise 75% of the global workforce by 2025 will also bring about changes. Despite all of their "connectedness" and the digital capability of the millennial generation, there is often a noticeable lack of employee engagement in the workplace. Your leadership team needs to understand this group of workers behavior in order to get your full team properly prepared and amped to be victorious in your packaged application rollout and in all business processes. You will need to capture the imagination and loyalty of this generation of workers and leverage their important new skills, ideas and energy to help your company succeed-now and in the future.

With multiple examples and years of research, the book "Gen Y Now, Millennials and the Evolution of Leadership", shares how to be an effective 21st century leader and deal with Gen Y. Co-Authored by Buddy Hobart and Herb Sendek, it is a great source of insight on engaging millennials. For college basketball fans, it is worth noting that Herb Sendek is the current NCAA basketball coach at Santa Clara, coached James Harden at Arizona State and also competed and coached against tobacco road rivals and perennial national contenders University of North Carolina (UNC) and Duke, while coaching at North Carolina State University, where he won ACC coach of the year.

The book provides some background on the importance of the Gen Yers. Gen Y refers to those people born between 1977 and 1995. In addition to being the most well-educated generation of all time, starting in 2013, every 8 seconds for the next eighteen years, a Gen Yer will turn 36. They are fully immersed within our teams and workforce. Gen Y, with its 80 million members, is the future of work. By 2025, 75% of the global workforce will be Gen Y and a significant part of the remaining 25% will be the generation following Gen Y.

Some common myths and misperceptions exist which older generations have of Gen Yers. As the book points out, "Many Baby Boomers and Generation Xers are quick to stereotype Millennials as entitled, self-absorbed and lacking the work ethic of previous generations. But research has shown these common biases to be incorrect. Failing to recognize the tremendous assets of Generation Y could do irreparable damage to your company in the years to come." Millennials are problem solvers, tech savvy and think globally.

The ability for coaches to unite and inspire players to perform at a higher level is fundamental to competing in sports and is only possible when true leadership is present. Your leadership and change management teams need to be armed and prepared to address multi-generational issues. A key first step in an effective change management approach is acknowledging and including any multi-generational differences that might exist in the scope of the project work within the project change management plan. The overall corporate change management strategy on this should also be considered. Once the issues are noted, the details understood and analyzed, the appropriate change management tools can be applied. For example, as part of the project kickoff or other project communication vehicles, the change management team can survey and share perceptions that each generation has of the other generations and use facts (and humor) to start to break down the barriers that might exist.

Super Users - Key Change Agents

Super users (SU) are very vital to the change management effort. They receive a lot of attention in this chapter. The super users are project team members identified by their business process owners (BPOs) and drawn from the business team. They serve as key subject matter expertise with a deep understanding of their respective business processes. These team members should be the best and brightest from your business team as they will critical to design and be carrying the torch of knowledge for the packaged application going forward. The project knowledge transition plan from the external consultants to the SU is a focus area in winning the ERP and packaged application game. Many clients fail to require that this knowledge transition activity be called out clearly in the project implementation plan with their SI and fail to include it in the phase exit criteria to assure it is happening or is confirmed by the SUs. Business SUs should be confirming effective knowledge transitioning, and this is another key to winning the game.

Supers users own many of the ERP and packaged application responsibilities in assuring that the Business and the IT team are aligned. SUs are responsible for (1) being a business process subject matter expert when the packaged application solution capabilities are assessed and blueprinted for the future to-be process. This assessment should involve a strong collaboration with the global BPO and identifying gaps that will prevent the business from being successful. The SUs have to be forward thinking with a clear understanding that not using the out-of-the-box application capabilities will result in initial and on-going incremental costs to the business. This out-of-the-box option is balanced against the business's factual, not perceived, ability to meet vital and market differentiating needs to serve the customer.

Another responsibility of the SU is (2) business testing and user acceptance testing (UAT) of the solution. This testing applies to both the initial project implementation and subsequent new change requirements. They also provide input to business process governance for on-going changes in the application that are managed through the change control board (CCB) mentioned in Chapter 3.

The SUs also have the responsibility of (3) training the rest of your business process end users. A Best Practice is to align your business SUs with the external consultants to accelerate SU learning as part of the overall train the trainer (TTT) activity whereby the SU are trained to deliver the end user training. The degree of staff augmentation with external consultants can be as-needed, based upon the effectiveness of the on-going SU knowledge acquisition process and bandwidth of the SU team. It is in the best interest of your business to have your SU use the TTT requirement as an opportunity to further ramp up their packaged application knowledge.

The final responsibility discussed that the SU role owns is that of first point of contact (FPOC) for other users during the go-live and subsequent business-as-usual operations. End users should be instructed to first contact the super user with any questions so that issues can be identified and worked as close to the action as possible. The SU can work the resolution and root cause analysis with the IT team.

A key point on the number of super users required per process. As part of the SU identification process, BPOs need to manage the ratio of SU to end users across geographies and language barriers. Effective ratios of SU to end user are vital to quality end user training and support. A Best Practice within the on-going ratio management process includes SU attrition planning and new SU boarding since the business should plan for on-going SU roles. People in SU roles move on for a variety of reasons including well deserved promotions and jettisoning the company for greener pastures elsewhere. I was working with a major international company that had a large go-live in China and one of the business process teams lost nearly 50% of their SU due to attrition within the first 12 months of go-live as the local SU were leaving the company for opportunities to increase their salaries by nearly 50-60% with their newly acquired ERP skillset. The business did not plan for this and it caused serious disruption to the business process and to the demands on the remaining SU, as they became overloaded with all of the extra holes they had to fill.

Coaching Moment – Project implementation and on-going knowledge transition activities to your SUs should be a key metric and the business process owners and project management should monitor it closely.

Coaching Moment – Plan for boarding of new SU and anticipate attrition, especially in emerging growth markets and hot skill areas. Make sure your HR team is engaged early to help respond to market demands and improve retention.

Empowering Your Super User/End User Community

As part of the "super user/end user" community you should establish, a culture of self-empowerment and self-governing to drive ongoing value realization should be created. Providing the users tools and processes to enable this are critical. There are a number of ways to assess user adoption of the packaged application. One proven way is by seeing how many manual process activities supporting rework happen. There are several approaches that can be used to monitor the rework activity. With the major advances in technologies and platform performance with cloud and in-memory databases, automated data analysis views can be made available to the users so they can easily self-assess and self-govern their performance and can now leverage this data to drive self-empowerment and governance. Users can view opportunity areas for improvement. A user can be provided with data and information to see how they are performing in the system. This can be used to help coach and drive a proactive behavior from the user.

We will talk more about powerful data analytics tools later in the book beyond just the people/culture dimension of your transformation initiative. We will share other specific examples and ways which these tools have been used to deliver innovation and improve business processes, operations monitoring, overall governance and value realization. These analytics tools truly are game changing as they offer an ease of use not previously available for deep real time insight into how your business is running, ways to improve it and then measure how effectively your changes are working.

Business Adoption Rate

The business adoption rate of the packaged application rollout is a key metric to winning the game. Raising the business adoption rate is paramount to a successful ERP project and getting value realized. The higher you raise the adoption rate the likely the higher the value realized by your business. There are two main impact groups we will discuss, the change leaders, and the end users of the solution. Change leaders are the key people that are your champions for change. This group includes stakeholders and the super users. Stakeholders, due to the significant impact from the outcome of the ERP project they receive, and their leadership roles, must become strong advocates. Within the plans for raising the business adoption rate we discuss next, we develop specific OCM management plans and activities for both the stakeholders and super users. We can't overstate the importance of both of these groups becoming effective change agents and among the project's biggest fans.

Per Figure 4, we see how over the duration of the project, we drive up the business adoption rate. First, we engage the change leaders and drive up their level of adoption from "awareness" to "understanding" to "acceptance" to "commitment". Second, for the end users, and through interaction with the change leaders, we raise the end user level of adoption. We achieve this by executing the key workstreams within the "organizational change", "communications" and "training" groupings in the Business Adoption Key Workstream Examples, Figure 5.

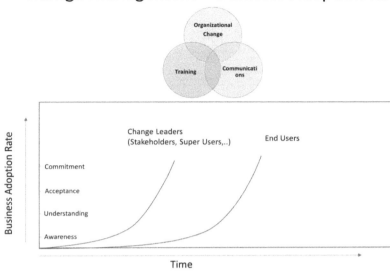

Figure 4- Business Adoption Rate

Raising the Business Adoption Rate

Figure 5 identifies key OCM workstreams to help raise your company's business adoption rate mapped across an example methodology. It is not meant to be a full listing of all workstreams that are exercised throughout a packaged application project. Let's categorize the OCM activities into three key buckets/groupings. "organizational change", "communications" and "training". Applicable templates, tools, Best Practices and lessons learned discussed here are available for your team within methodologies to accelerate the successful rollout and execution of these workstreams. You can also augment your team with coaching from an advisory consultant, as needed, to improve your team's self-sufficiency in driving the business adoption rate.

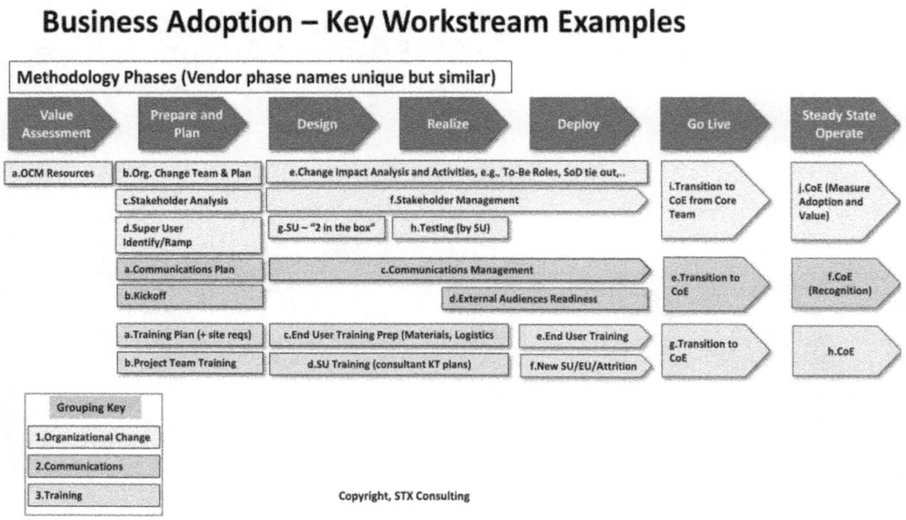

Business Adoption – Key Workstream Examples

Figure 5- Key Workstreams Driving Business Adoption

Below is brief description of each grouping and workstream:

(1) Organizational Change Grouping: Change management – focused on organization change leadership, roles (to-be process, RACI, BPO and organizational resource/funding alignment, stakeholders and super users as key change agents, value realization management….)

a) **OCM Resources** – Initial qualification of OCM skills and abilities within the organization to participate. Additionally, initial engagement of OCM leader in alignment on value assessment organization change strategic impact.

b) **Organizational Change Team and Plan** – Assemble organizational change leadership to develop an overall organization change plan to support the packaged application project plan. This plan should include post-production transition of tasks to the CoE.

c) **Stakeholder Analysis** – The objective of this task is to establish the stakeholder management plan which includes identification and analysis of the stakeholders.

d) **Super User Identification/Ramp** – Identify the super users for the project and begin to ramp them on the project team and knowledge curve.

e) **Change Impact Analysis and Activities**, e.g., "to-be" roles, SoD tie out. - As part of the to-be process activity, new roles that are identified need to be socialized with the business to assess impact, e.g., additional funding required, which roles might disappear, initial segregation of duties (SoD) assessment, authorizations, and RACI charts created (Responsible/Accountable/Consulted/Involved). This is a key activity and it is essential to start this analysis as early as possible to avoid last minute surprises.

f) **Stakeholder Management** – As part of the early stakeholder analysis (plan), this is the on-going management of the stakeholders and should be taking place to assure on-going buy-in and early identification of any issues or concerns being raised. The on-going collaboration and dialogue throughout the project with the stakeholders are invaluable to getting a true view of the good and the bad on how things are being received within the user community and actions needed.

g) **Super User (SU) "2-in-the-box"** – Super users should be tightly coupled with the packaged application SI consultants and be immersing themselves via a "2-in-the-box" approach with the consultants to achieve knowledge transfer. This is on-going and should be one of the workstreams readying the super user to conduct the solution testing. In this example, "2-in-the-box" refers to the close working relationship between the consultant(s) and super users.

h) **Testing (by Super User (SU))**- As part of the process of transferring knowledge to the Super users, the SUs should conduct the integration and end to end testing (not unit test done by developers). The super users should work very

closely with the packaged application consultant within
testing to assure knowledge transfer takes place from the SI
consulting team to the super user team.

i) **Transition to the CoE from the Core Team**-As part of the
project transitioning from project phase into operational
mode, your CoE should be the team that takes over on-
going program related organizational change activities. If
your organization has a dedicated organizational change
team outside of the CoE, a collaborative working model
should be established.

j) **CoE Measure Adoption and Value**- Measuring the
adoption and value should be institutionalized as part of
the CoE's responsibility during the normal operations
phase of the program, since the CoE is the team that will
remain in place to support your packaged application into
the foreseeable future. To draw on sports analogies,
establishing "personal bests" and "team bests" as part of the
measurement workstream is a Best Practice. Data analytics
provide a great tool to quantify personal and team
performance. The topic of data analytics will be discussed
more later in the book. Friendly competitions using the
right coaching can add fun and motivation to driving
increased team performance.

(2) <u>Communications Grouping</u>: Communicating on all fronts
and channels across the business to make sure as many people as
possible are aware of what the status of the project is and what is being
asked of them and helping to answer questions.

a) **Communications Plan**- This is the communication plan for
the project. You can address specific needs here also. This
includes communications with internal and external
groups, e.g., customers, vendors, partners. For example,
some of your key business roles may be exercised by
subcontractors. Given the growing role of the "gig
economy" and freelancers, it may be prudent to determine
how best to communicate with these team members since
they may be representing your brand.

b) **Kickoff**-This is the project kickoff with the project team where you cover the "Who/What/Why/Where/When and How" overview of the project with the team to bring everyone up to a common baseline understanding.

c) **Communications Management**-This is managing and executing the communication plan activities and tasks.

d) **External Audiences Readiness**-The communications plan should include communications with your external audiences such as customers and suppliers at the appropriate times for their awareness and education, if needed.

e) **Transition to CoE**-This is the transition of the communication responsibility to the CoE to carry on the communications after the project team has completed the project.

f) **CoE (Recognition)**-As part of post go-live and on-going project successes, the communications responsibility in the CoE should include driving recognition and awards for deserving team members to celebrate successes visibly. The project communications team can also drive recognition during the project implementation phases. Attrition and retainment plans should be put in place with HR to avoid losing top players through free agency, including super users.

(3) **Training Grouping**: Training of all the team members, business users and stakeholders to satisfy their knowledge level to successfully operate the packaged application confidently to meet the business needs. There are many commercial tools to help with developing and/or delivering training. These tools also range in price and complexity. Many are now being made available via the cloud with a subscription to cut down on the initial license cost. The tool(s) selected depend on the Culture, budget and long-term strategy.

a) **Training Plan (plus site requirements)** -This is the overall training plan that covers training for all of those requiring it, e.g., super users, project team, stakeholders, end users. It should include any site-specific requirements to be worked out with the local extended team. It should address the content, channels for delivery, audience size and location. Taking advantage of social media technology is a way to add innovation and creativity to your plan, e.g., the use of YouTube as an option for educational training tools and self-study can become an excellent platform upon which to build.

b) **Project Team Training**-This is the training of the project team on the overall project. The project kickoff is usually a good introduction to the project and answers the who, why, what, where, when and how questions.

c) **End User Training Prep (Materials, Logistics..)**-These are the preparation activities for end user training and includes developing the content (classroom, web based, self-guided, online help,...), infrastructure and logistics plans (rooms, locations to map the multiple sites,...). End user training is often delivered by the super user team with support, as needed, from SI consultants. It also reinforces the need (and Best Practice) for an effective knowledge transfer (KT) transition plan from the consultants to the super user.

d) **Super User (SU) Training (Consultants Knowledge Transfer (KT) plans)**-Super user training activities are critical activities as the SUs from the business team are key change leaders and they need to be empowered through knowledge to carry the message forward. If the SUs are confident and comfortable with the solution, that bodes well for them transferring knowledge to end users and the SU becoming a strong change agent. The consultant knowledge transfer (KT) to the super user is a vital component of the super user training. The super user KT activity should include ways to optimize and continually enhance the SUs knowledge, including establishing communities, networks and leveraging professional organizations like Industry User Groups, e.g., Americas SAP User Group (ASUG).

e) **End User Training**-The end users of the solution all need to be effectively trained and ready to go prior to the go-live. This is a very sizeable task and another critical success factor.

f) **New Super Users(SU)/End Users(EU) and Attrition** – It is important that prior to go-live, a process needs to be put in place, working with the business process owners, to identify and board new SUs, to board new end users and be able to deal with SU and end-user attrition. Encourage business process owners to be proactive here to allow a quick response and backfill to the appropriate SU staffing levels required to support the business.

g) **Transition to the CoE**-The training responsibility should transition to the CoE sustainment team as the project team ramps down. This includes keeping the super users engaged and educated on new capabilities that are being planned for future enhancement rollouts. The core project team and the CoE team should put a transition plan in place so that this transition is a smooth activity.

h) **CoE**-The CoE owns the training responsibility for maintaining and enhancing the existing training materials, delivery channels and on-going plans.

OCM Governance

OCM governance includes how to apply processes, tools, lessons learned and Best Practices to the people/culture dimension of your packaged application transformation. Challenges and ways to address those, including the critical operate/sustain phase with its prominent role in value realization, are worth noting. Innovative approaches on the data analytics front can give you insight into your business adoption rate that was not previously easily possible. Applying these tools of quantitative monitoring wisely can enable a team through self-empowerment and self-governance toward improvement by viewing collective peer and individual benchmarked performance.

OCM workstream success through creative and realtime governance is much more feasible today than it was even five years ago. Governance from the PMO based on proactive monitoring and management of each of the workstreams is required. When a workstream starts to come off the rails or run into challenges or issues, the PMO needs to be ready to respond quickly. It may even require the PMO reaching across to the executive steering committee to address a larger organizational challenge that requires top level communications or Board level decisions. It is imperative to resolve change management interference as soon as it starts to surface. We have all seen how negative emotions can infect a much larger audience very quickly. Using tools for effective communications, resistance management, training and education of both change leaders and end users and on-going governance, can enable a much higher rate of business adoption.

A Best Practice is to assess your project OCM governance maturity to provide insight into improvement areas. A governance assessment typically covers all of the pillars of transformation; people/culture (OCM and business adoption), business processes and technology. By using a blend of qualitative and quantitative rating analysis, results can indicate maturity Level 1 (immature) to Level 5 (very mature). These results can be used to help gauge how effective your OCM governance is at any point in time. This provides baseline data upon which you can make plans to improve. For reference, there is more discussion on the governance maturity assessment process in Chapter 5 with an example provided for the business process pillar.

Chapter 5 – The Playbook – Business Processes and Master Data

"If you can't describe what you are doing as a process, you don't know what you're doing."

W. Edwards Deming, the quality guru and evangelist. He helped the Japanese industrial engine return to prominence after World War II and helped US corporations adopt quality controls across all aspects of the business.

A business process is a logically related set of activities that defines how specific business tasks are performed. Business processes are the ways in which organizations coordinate and organize work activities, knowledge and information to produce their products and/or services.

How well a business performs depends on how well its business processes are designed and executed. Business processes that are designed well can be a source of competitive advantage for a company if it can use the processes to innovate or perform with greater agility than its competitors. This is foundational to operational excellence. Conversely, poorly designed and/or executed business processes can be a liability if they are based on outdated ways of working or outdated technology and impede responsiveness, capability or efficiency.

Poorly designed processes can also introduce a host of controls risks that sabotage the business. On one project I recommended to the program supply chain executive that the to-be process documentation, which was being reused from an earlier pilot project, was of little value to the super users and stakeholders to review. It didn't reflect their processes. The pilot project process documentation should have been redone and updated to reflect the complexities of the larger site's processes. This would provide many obvious benefits including a more accurate understanding to the business of what was coming and enable a better process design discussion, with feedback for improvements before go-live. The executive decided that this recommendation was not needed, and the poor design approach proceeded. The go-live was a disaster with order delivery disruptions, a decline in customer service levels and significant lost sales over a significant time period.

The business process pillar is another foundational element to value realization. Whatever packaged software application you are implementing, a business process view of the initiative is vital to the approach. As a first step, ask yourself, "Are there clear global and/or regional business process owners (BPOs) defined in my organization and are they authorized to make the needed business decisions to enable the desired process transformation?" If not, then take the steps needed to make this happen. A good next step if these roles are missing or largely paper roles with no teeth, is to engage your OCM leadership to drive top executive buy-in to help to identify and empower the process owners. Transforming your processes, organization and technology to realize harmonized global to-be processes that are truly adopted by the business are key to not only initial value realization but, even more importantly, to sustaining and building on the benefits. BPOs play an instrumental role in governing the changes needs to be successful.

The business process scope also comes into play when aiming for success. ERP implementations at many companies often stall or deliver less than expected because of the complexity of the legacy environment and getting organizations to simplify without deeming every little business unit nuance of a legacy process as vital to the new to-be processes. These nuances usually drive customization and some companies have thousands of Workflow, Report, Interface, Conversion, Enhancement and Form (WRICEF) requests requiring custom development. Right off the bat, the PMO and any senior oversight committee should say "No" to that mindset and enforce an "out-of-the-box" packaged application philosophy. If the business unit(s) can't simplify the processes, the likelihood of transforming to a better and more nimble company is almost certainly derailed. A governance Best Practice is to place the onus and burden of on-going customization costs onto those demanding it directly or at least calling the annual incremental costs out separately and allocating those costs to those business process owners. Making somebody responsible for funding the added custom developed activities is a good way to determine how critical the customizations are to that business unit. There are often some customizations that are truly justified, and the governance process should address those unique needs without embracing every request. The change request management process and change control board should always consider cost/value/risk while asking "why not out-of-the-box"?

The case of many packaged application customizations surfacing and being required might warrant determining whether a smaller scope is more appropriate to establish a basic new process footprint for better determining future needs. One tradeoff with a smaller new footprint is the number of legacy applications and custom interfaces that will need to be developed and maintained if the ERP scope is reduced, relying on legacy applications until some future rollout point. This "transition" architecture will add a level of complexity and support required to operate the business until the full scope is implemented. Also, how you implement that "transition" architecture and to what degree it is easy to decouple from and move to the full ERP scope, is an added element to be fully understood. Interfaces are an area requiring strong business process ownership governance. First, in deciding if the custom interface is required and if so, how it can be simplified and then how it can be effectively operated and managed. More on the interface topic in Chapter 6.

Enterprise Process Framework

As you define the scope of the project, a good starting point is a review of your enterprise process framework. The enterprise process framework is an end to end enterprise view of all of the business processes within your company. If this view doesn't exist, a good starting point is a reference business process model to provide valuable insight into your enterprise process structure. The American Productivity & Quality Center (APQC) Process Classification Framework (PCF) provides such models. As their website states, "The PCF is a list of universal business processes performed by every business, giving you a common language to communicate and define work processes across your organization." APQC has a library of PCFs by industry in addition to their cross-industry PCF.

When you have the process framework of the enterprise in place, it becomes an excellent reference point for multiple analyses. Mapping all applications across your process framework provides valuable insight in analyzing the operating costs that each process and or sub process drives. Which processes should be in scope for the packaged application implementation and whether those processes are unique and differentiating for competitive advantage or not is also another characteristic that can be added to your process framework mapping. Heat maps, an example is shown in Chapter 7, Figure 10, can be drawn based upon different criteria as part of the analysis. Once you have identified the processes in scope, the legacy applications that are used to operate those processes today and whether there is anything unique and differentiating to those sub-processes for competitive advantage, enables you to begin to perform a high level value assessment, gap fit and refine the proposed scope of the packaged application.

Legacy Applications

As part of the process for legacy application mapping, you can identify which processes and applications are truly transforming the business versus those that are largely in operate or run mode. The more you can invest in the transform part of the business the better as that is where the innovation and market differentiation should be happening.

Over time, the "transform" applications of today will evolve into the "run" applications of tomorrow. New transform initiatives will be generated while all the applications should be continually optimized. It is a Best Practice that you have a clear view of where and how your business dollars are funding your innovation and transform business process workstreams. This run vs transform investment will be covered in Chapter 7, Value Realization.

Process Simplification

Process simplification thinking should take place by process owners and the business as part of the up-front value assessment. I have seen many projects doom themselves by missing simplification opportunities because the work is too difficult or the effort might possibly delay the start of the ERP project. It is easier for companies to (heavily) customize their ERP implementations and create a burden of technical debt rather than simplify complex processes. Attempting process simplification can involve lengthy and extensive global debates about what pieces of a business process are differentiating and essential. Concerns are raised that without the custom code, it may cause customer satisfaction issues. These design discussions can often become prolonged and pose a threat to the project timeline (and executive bonuses), hence the path of least resistance decision is to incur the technical debt. The lack of transparent and objective as-is business processes contributes heavily in these discussions. I experienced one customer running into significant project delays due to the lack of progress on fulfilment process design simplification discussions and identifying the true customer needs. The leadership team, in desperation to move forward, finally ended up approving the porting of hundreds of thousands of lines of legacy fulfilment custom code onto the new target ERP solution, saddling the new project with a crippling amount of technical debt.

Once ERP is installed, it usually has a long life of use within your business so keep that in mind when making process simplification decisions. It puzzles me how someone can think that there is not enough time to simplify the process beforehand and end up building in significant complexity into the ERP system enabled business processes that will last another ten to twenty plus years!

I suspect that as you see the topic of process simplification, you will immediately think of processes within your business that seem overly complex to your team or your customers. You may have even heard your customers state this or people within your team ask, "why does this have to be so complex"? Let me share examples of opportunities to simplify.

A good example that I have seen is product structure complexity. Rather than simplify the product structure and related process, clients incorporate complex product structures without first examining if there is a way to simplify this structure. For some this complexity may require the use of variant configuration (VC) structures. This VC complexity permeates all ends of the business from customer facing quoting and order management, through planning, manufacturing and procurement. This complexity may certainly be warranted and needed for some businesses and if so, skip to the next paragraph. However, for some it seems to just happen because it is just the way it has always been. In one software firm, they had software offering bill of materials (BoM) that looked like a BoM for a commercial jetliner. Never did they entertain the idea of exploring simplification. When I raised the recommendation, the program executive shared that she was concerned that there was not enough time to go through a product structure simplification activity and meet the ERP program timeline. To quote the legendary Hall of Fame UCLA college basketball coach John Wooden, "If you don't have time to do it right you must have time to do it over." The customer's project incurred several significant delays with master data extract-translate-load (ETL) challenges being one of the major contributors and after go-live, it caused very high end-to-end process complexity for years.

At another client, variant configuration was required for part of their business while other lines of business did not need it, yet their Big Four consulting firm advised them to use variant configuration across all business lines. As part of a post go-live advisory consulting engagement, I advised the business unit leadership that we could simplify this process by simply making nearly all of the products standard offerings (variants). By going this route, much of the end to end process complexity associated with variant configuration dynamics and creating top level items from many variant subassemblies and parts on the fly, was removed. Using a specific variant in a one-for-one arrangement simplified their business processes significantly. One startup PC maker exploited the idea of the variant stockable products early on in the PC industry to avoid the complexity and costs needed for supporting every possible configuration known by limiting the options to a few key features which customers desired. This idea propelled them to become one of the dominant global PC makers. This product simplification approach translated into many process simplification steps, allowed them to command a significant part of the PC market by being first mover and forced the other players to catch up to them.

In another example, using complex planning strategy models through advanced planning and optimization modules may not be something you are ready to include in scope, especially if your people and culture are not prepared for them. These modules are great and can do a great job of planning and optimizing the supply and demand data, if you are ready and properly prepared with these advanced planning skills to operate and digest the data. If on the other hand, your team struggles with less complex planning approaches, it is warranted to take a closer look at the change effort required and how to get there. I have seen many clients struggle significantly with getting these sophisticated planning modules to operate routinely. I have asked customers struggling with their newly installed advanced planning strategies if they were successfully running MRP beforehand, which is a much simpler planning approach, and a common reply was that they were not really using MRP beforehand even though they had that capability. This is likely a red flag that got discounted somehow when scope was being decided. Maybe they didn't truly understand their existing process and organizational capabilities or overestimated their team's ability to adopt the new complex process tools given their starting point. Your change management team really needs to look for situations like this, raise flags and put plans in place to address the gaps.

We also have the situation where the customer was using a pricing model for their offerings that had its origins in very complex product structures going back a number of years. A story being shared was that this pricing model and its complexity was in place because, in the past, they wanted their customers to have to engage the sales team to get pricing information to enable upselling. The products and general business model in the industry had become much simpler for clients to understand, yet this particular customer continued to suffer with this complex pricing model that effectively was applied to many of the products that were developed. It was unable to break down the cultural barriers because many of the existing leaders had grown up with that complex pricing process and it was considered a badge of pride. There is a reason many experts say that "change is hard".

Jeff Bezos and his Amazon team have taken numerous historically complex processes and simplified them. For example, even something as complex as the infrastructure and application hosting with all of the moving parts of technology involved in the different solutions offered, Amazon introduced the standard on how to deliver this complexity with a straight forward approach, simplifying multiple aspects of the process including pricing. Amazon has benefited immensely from first market mover to providing simplified customer experiences for cloud offerings (Amazon Web Services (AWS)). Other technology companies were in the cloud business before Amazon, but Amazon took the model and made it easily digestible for customers, Customers rewarded Amazon as they became the dominant force in cloud offerings. It is one of the Amazon trademarks of their innovation and creativity, taking existing business models and simplifying them to remove complexity. They transform the processes in to a seamless and smooth customer experience, easily understood from purchasing to paying to receiving their product or service.

Businesses continue to look for ways to add value and differentiate themselves in the marketplace. As you assess your business processes and the degree that these processes are unable to "fit" to the standard out-of-the-box processes in the packaged application, you need to ask the question of how does this uniqueness being requested differentiate my business? Do customers do business with me because of that uniqueness? Do my internal operations benefit significantly from this? Is there some competitive advantage that is being driven by this uniqueness? Or, is the root of the uniqueness tied to "we have always done it that way" or "we can't really quantify the value it provides"? These questions should surface many times when businesses take a hard look at the "fit-gap" analysis when assessing the standard process capabilities offered by many packaged applications against raised requirements. Strong governance with a focus on process simplification needs to be exercised.

Differentiating vs Non-Differentiating Processes

As part of your business process mapping activity, you should identify differentiating and non-differentiating processes.

- Differentiating: You have business processes which are truly differentiating. Your company is the only one that adds this "secret sauce" or produces that type of product or service. This is what makes you special to your customers.
- Non-Differentiating: These business processes are just standard business processes. Your customers don't view this as unique and differentiating. You either operate the same as the competition in that area or your customers just don't see any added value to that element. These are ideal candidates for out-of-the-box packaged application processes and/or outsourcing.

Differentiating processes and the ability to execute better than your competitors are your secret sauce to satisfying your customers. Differentiation is often based upon the process of distinguishing a product or service from others and the unique processes involved in enabling the difference. These differences must be valued by your customers. There are many examples of commodity products combined with offering strategic unique customer experiences and services that have led to successful differentiation in the marketplace.

These differentiating processes can drive business decisions around customization of the packaged application or extending your architecture by adding a "best of breed" application to address it. You may address this in your business IT landscape by justified application customization or inserting a "best of breed" bolt-on application within your architecture. This will drive up initial and on-going solution costs. It is imperative to (1) determine if the desired capability is truly differentiating in the eyes of your customers and/or your business operations and, if it is, (2) qualify the ROI on the differentiating capability to make sure the benefits justify the "gap" in the packaged application that needs to be addressed.

If customization or inserting a "best of breed" application to the project are deemed warranted, when performing the ROI, make sure to include not just the one-time initial development/purchase costs but also the increased costs associated with supporting the customization and/or maintaining the bolt-on package over the life of the solution. Adding complex customization or a complex interface will likely extend the project timeline and increase the risk. Additional testing, training, supplier management and other project tasks with their added costs are very likely.

Another long-term impact from using more customization is your annual "run" versus "transform" dollar ratio. Whatever your IT transform/run spend ratio is, every organization's goal is to spend more on transforming and innovating the business versus operating and running the existing systems. Building in more customization and complexity are going to drive up the run costs for the solution after it is operational. Business process owners need to consider this point as well since they will see fewer dollars available for future innovation as a result of the customization they approve now. We will discuss the transform/run IT spend ratio a bit more in Chapter 7 on value realization when we discuss total cost of ownership (TCO).

A process tool that has come to the forefront as a differentiating necessity is data analytics. Data analytics are shaking up multiple industries, and the effects are becoming more pronounced with the wide adoption of data analytics. This trend will continue to grow at an unprecedented fashion. More and more data is available. Data volumes continue to double at a rapid rate as data pours in from multiple sources, e.g., ERP and other IT applications, mobile phones, wireless sensors and IOT. Organizations that are able to harness these data analytics capabilities effectively will be able to create significant value and differentiate themselves, while others will find themselves increasingly at a disadvantage. The topic of data analytics will get more discussion later.

Master Data Management (MDM)

MDM is one of the most critical ingredients in getting your new business processes to work with your packaged software and likely one of the most challenging to pull together.

What is master data and why does it play such a critical role? In simplest terms, master data is data about your customers, products, suppliers, personnel and financials that gets combined with your business rules to drive the new transactions and to-be business processes. **Master data + business rule setup (application configuration) = business transactions**. The business transactions are the backbone of your packaged application enabled business processes, e.g., Create Purchase Requisition, Create Purchase Order, Receive Goods, Receive Invoice, Pay Invoice. The product and supplier data that populates these purchasing transaction examples originates in the Master Data you create in the packaged application.

Trusted and consistent master data is a prerequisite for flawless business processes and reliable enterprise analytics. This holds true for on-premise and hybrid landscapes. If your ERP and IT applications are built on flawed master data such as errant customer or product data, the proliferation of that bad data within your data warehouses is fast and difficult to go back and clean up. In addition to the proliferation of bad data, it causes problems in carrying out your day to day ERP transactions, e.g., Sales Orders, Purchase Orders, Production Orders. Enabling a successful foundation for transacting business and analyzing the results is built on high quality and reliable master data management.

Many organizations have a regional or line of business approach at managing master data without clear master data process ownership and governance. Other organizations have limited definition around how to manage master data. Often, products and new product introduction have some process structure in place since lines of business need this to introduce new products to market and this typically falls under the product lifecycle management (PLM) process. But other master data is often managed in an ad hoc manner.

Once enterprise master data management is identified by the business as something critical that needs to be managed and governed, establishing global process ownership, data stewards and governance should follow. In some cases, the effort to get the data ready for use can be daunting. Duplicates usually exist and business rules need to be established as part of the governance process to remove the duplicates and cleanse the errant data while keeping the data clean going forward. In a number of organizations, getting to the people who can help define some of the key data values can be a challenge. For example, I have worked with several customers challenged with obtaining good safety stock values for their raw material master data. Either the previous values didn't exist, or the data was bad. Getting to the manufacturing experts to help define these values can be difficult for a variety of reasons. There may be alternatives but getting manufacturing experts to validate is always a Best Practice. Collaborative process ownership and governance is essential.

In the case of the SAP packaged application suite, moving to SAP HANA from ECC will offer a unique opportunity to clean up business partner data because it requires moving from the "legacy" customer and vendor master data records to the to-be "business partner" master data. This conversion offers a chance that should be embraced by the business to clean up the legacy ECC data as you move to S4 HANA.

The packaged application software suppliers often offer applications to help clean up the master data via business rules that you can define, and they can offer data governance applications to help with on-going data governance. These applications are transformational just like your other packaged applications and you will need to establish a to-be process with to-be roles and ownership to effectively use them. These applications are also not a panacea and are typically augmented with other processes like business data standards management.

Master data governance tools should enable a user-friendly framework and architecture supporting materials, suppliers, customers, ledger accounts, profit centers, cost elements, personnel records and other key master data. The framework should enable a single trusted source for the data that can be shared among your entire business application landscape, e.g., ERP, CRM, SCM. Workflow capabilities are required to route data for creation and updates (CRUD – Create, Read, Update, Delete) and approval by the appropriate stakeholders, data stewards and process owners. As part of the governance engine, validation functions are also needed. The framework should provide services and an application programming interface (API) so customers can extend the framework flexibly.

There are multiple aspects to the master data that are used to measure and monitor data quality. Aspects are listed below with customer master data related examples:

- **Accuracy**: Determines the extent to which data objects correctly represent the real-world values for which they were designed Example: Customer title and address must be correct.
- **Completeness**: Determines the extent to which required data is not missing, e.g., tax codes.
- **Conformity**: Determines the extent to which data conforms to a specified format.
  Example: Customer postal code is in the correct format
- **Consistency**: Determines the extent to which distinct data instances provide non-conflicting information about the same underlying data object.
- **Integrity**: Determines the extent to which data is not missing important relationship linkages.
- **Uniqueness**: Determines the extent to which data is not duplicated. Example: The customer name and address should be unique for each customer. Cross referencing customer record

creation by verifying via an industry accepted ID like DUNS number can help eliminate duplicates.

- **Up to date (Timely)**: Determines the extent to which data is sufficiently up to date.

Data cleansing is a top concern for many companies. Many have inconsistent or nonexistent cleansing policies today that lead to poor data quality. The more siloed teams and systems are due to a lack of collaboration between IT and the business, the greater the risk for inaccurate data and multiple sources for master data. It is not that unusual for a company without strong data governance to discover that master data has been wrong for months or longer. Poor quality data is a high-risk scenario that stymies innovation. It is important to build an effective master data management process and then build your layers of added value on top. Otherwise, you can expect poor results.

As part of any master data cleanup and governance effort, business rules are often defined and applied to the master data to help cleanse it as it is migrated or transformed into your packaged application. Some examples of rules used to clean up customer master data and remove duplicates are shown below:

- Check that the fields have valid values.
- Check that fields are unique if required, e.g., VAT number, customer name.
- Check that the DUNS number is unique for a given business partner.
- Check that values follow any adopted naming schemes for a given field.
- Check that the correct relationships are in place, e.g., are the correct ship-to party(s), bill-to, mapped to correct sold-to partner.
- Check that the right language values are set up on the customer records for printing needed output.
- Check that valid postal code values are used.
- Check that the correct country codes are used for given cities.
- Check for inactive customer records to determine if these are valid or should be removed, e.g., no transaction history for the given customer since the system went live five years ago.
- Check for completeness of the master data record.

Business Data Standards

What are business data standards (BDS) and how do you govern them? Think of these standards as the core set of agreed values that can populate a field so that the value entered matches within the scope of what the global business expects (also referred to as check table technology within the application). As part of BDS, data stewards are identified as the keeper of the values that are permitted to be used. For example, only agreed company code (legal entity) values are used. The BDS process typically includes workflow from the business requesting a value to the data steward for review and approval across the business to all subscribing and interested parties. Once the data steward approves the new value it is added to the packaged application check tables and the user can then create the value agreed upon. Changes to pre-existing values need extra governance to minimize the business impact of those changes and in some cases, these changes may warrant a mass change exercise on pre-existing data. The value of BDS becomes even more highly valuable when there are multiple packaged application solutions in place and the business is trying to consolidate or integrate across solutions. If different BDS exist for the same entity, data mapping/conversion tasks must resolve the differences.

The foundation of data analytics and effective ERP and packaged applications are quality master data. ERP and packaged applications are where your business processes run and historical data are essentially created for every aspect of your business. Without the quality master data for the ERP solutions, there is no source of data to mine. For example, if you have inadequate master data governance, users can create new materials even if the material master data already exists in the system. This results in not only bad data quality but also it generates unnecessary costs since every master data record has a cost to the business for its lifecycle. By implementing a business rule to check for duplicates, this improves data quality as well as business process quality and decision making. Master data governance and business data standards can help avoid data issues as early as possible. This saves time and money for the business and improves the quality on every subsequent activity built on top of that master data.

Business Process Data Analytics and Process Mining

With the advent of cloud, increased system performance and vast amounts of process event data within your packaged application, business process mining is emerging as a critical tool to get true transparency into your processes. There are also packages for raw data analytics if your needs are purely number crunching huge volumes of data. Taking data analytics to another level in the ERP and packaged application space for business process governance are the process data mining tools. These are **game changing** capabilities!

I have seen a number of projects that use data process mining tools and these tools truly are an order of magnitude improvement into process transparency and unleashing the value of your packaged application investment. First, by enabling discovery of how the software is being used to execute your processes today and then applying analysis, process enhancements, process automation and more to drive out the inefficiencies of your system or as process mining supplier Celonis touts, create the frictionless process.

Process mining can be applied before transformation to fully understand key as-is processes and benchmark against to-be processes, once those new processes are in place. It is not uncommon to hear companies talk about business process cycle times taking longer with their new ERP implementations than before they installed the new packaged application. Having the beforehand processes objectively documented can help shine a light on key current activities so you can understand where processes were previously working well and leveraging that knowledge to improve the to-be processes potentially.

Process mining provides business process X-ray vision capabilities to your business team to uncover how and why things are happening the way they are within your process. More on business process mining in Chapter 8.

Coaching Moment: As a Best Practice, your organization and your transformation efforts should be driven by a customer focused, business process led mindset with clear business process ownership to help drive the to-be processes or optimize the existing processes. Organizations with a business process mindset will immediately see that process mining is a tremendous tool to be

applied to your business process transformation. It can help drive process optimization and transparency in achieving operational excellence and your goals.

Business Processes and Automation

Many customers are already using or planning to use automation in their processes. This automation is typically implemented where there is no value add for a person to do tasks which can be done systematically. Reducing or removing human involvement from these processes will only work when companies are running those processes with clean data. Once these processes are automated and running, it allows your people (end users) to focus on more value-added activity

Process data analytics and process mining should be the first steps in enabling process automation. For example, process mining can be used to identify which business process tasks are ready to be automated and which ones aren't and suggest possible inhibitors to automation. There are numerous studies that associate billions of dollars of savings that could potentially be generated by robotic process automation. This topic will get discussed further in Chapter 8.

Business Process and Master Data Governance

Business process and master data governance can be reached with the Best Practices, tools, lessons learned and other insight shared here, to help you remove barriers to a successful packaged application based business transformation and move you along the road to success. Activities like alignment with strategy, process simplification and optimization and leveraging out-of-the-box packaged application process capabilities are vital to this governance.

The business process transformation that takes place with the implementation of the packaged software is the second pillar of the packaged application software effort. The process transformation needs to be aligned with the first pillar, organizational change management and the third pillar, technology. Foundational to a successful business process transformation is the business master data accuracy and correctness. Every future packaged application transaction you carry out will be based on this data. Get it wrong and your business will be feeling the pain for a long, long time before you can remedy it. Get it right, and a significant part of your business process transformation effort will be much simpler. Not only that, but get it right, and the value realization effort can be accelerated and amplified through data analytic process discovery and enhancement as well as process automation.

Governing your business process and master data activity and tasks will assure the proper implementation focus. Asking the right questions up front can help you focus on gaps to address and govern to avoid classic related pitfalls. Your packaged application supplier, SI and advisory consultant(s) should be working with you to guide your efforts here.

Below is a sample of some business process and master data governance analysis questions which I have used with customers to gauge their existing governing maturity and help guide them in achieving greater value realization of their business process and master data transformation efforts.

Question 1 – Are the company's IT decisions strategically aligned with the business needs?

Question 2 – Are clear business process and master data roles and responsibilities defined together with mutually agreed governance bodies and processes, including regular communication, with well-defined decision-making procedures?

Question 3 – Are business key performance indicators defined to measure the success of the business process execution and to detect deviations of the business process flow?

Question 4 – Are critical business processes technically analyzed (simplified) end to end, including interfaces, with a focus on meeting customers' needs, data consistency and performance?

Additional questions are customized to the customer.

These questions should be raised early in the project as part of the initial value assessment and at several checkpoint periods along the life cycle to assess your process governance maturity and if the change actions being applied are driving the desired results. The figure below illustrates the business process maturity KPI measurements. Monitoring and assessing how each of your transformational pillar efforts are doing can improve your governance and ultimate business results.

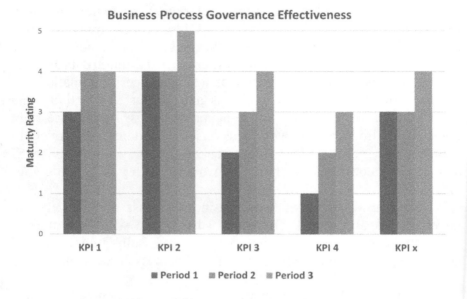

Figure 6- Quantifying Business Process Governance Effectiveness

The PMO along with business process owners need to drive this enterprise process governance and leverage the executive steering committee, as needed, to quickly get the business aligned around the governance model. Good governance means matching goals to data. Data analytics with process mining can provide very powerful tools to help strengthen governance and improve results. We will discuss leveraging data analytics and process mining further in Chapter 8

Chapter 6 – Technology

"We are stuck with technology when what we really want is just stuff that works."
Douglas Adams (Author -The Salmon of Doubt, The Hitchhiker's Guide to the Galaxy)

The technology is the platform and ecosystem made up of the software, infrastructure, technical consulting, partners, supplier support and methodologies to implement the packaged application solution and operate it.

As businesses compete and look for differentiating avenues to provide value to their customers, it is important that they can transact business with the customer smoothly end to end across their enterprise. From customer interaction CRM points to the backend ERP systems that process the sales orders and fulfill the ordered product or service efficiently across the supply chain while managing the financials and people, all enabled by packaged application technology. Packaged applications offer off-the-shelf business processes capable of satisfying many different business requirements.

Platform Infrastructure

The technology platform can reside on-premise, in the cloud or be a hybrid of both on-premise and cloud. The number of packaged application options being developed keeps increasing as technology evolves. Almost all of the latest packages leverage the cloud, though most vendors still offer an on-premise option for companies who still desire that option. The footprint across the business landscape of packaged application use will continue to grow. In addition, the cloud is a key enabler for generating the next wave of technology. Many of the new disruptive technologies such as artificial intelligence (AI), machine learning (ML), robotic process automation (RPA), internet of things (IoT) and virtual reality (VR), are now viable to many customers as a result of cloud technology. Cloud enables a scalable foundation for the creation of new business models very quickly. The message that we should expect to see more cloud technology adoption was reinforced by Hasso Plattner, one of SAP's original founders, at SAP's

SAPPHIRE customer event when he highlighted that the cloud is necessary to drive innovation.

Even with the flexibility, innovation, cost benefits and speed that the cloud enables, the technology adoption prerequisites of change management and effective governance are still present and, in many ways, will become even more critical and demanding. In order to compete and drive faster and faster business adoption and digestion of the rapidly evolving technology, incorporating a culture of change will be required. I have seen companies who preach a culture of change yet pay no credence to the need to formally have change management expertise and leaders on board to facilitate this cultural shift. Some companies struggle with where to locate these skills in their organization and others can't seem to justify the added expense for these "soft skills". I have shared some guidance earlier on OCM roles, leadership and insight. The cloud technology transition topic is a reinforcing point to emphasize how critical this OCM mindset is. If you don't have some form of OCM roles and processes on your team in place, plans should be made to do so, whether in-house or through staff augmentation and advisors. These OCM roles will help address several key transformation challenges to better prepare for the accelerating transformation demands that the cloud is driving. Note: Many of these same issues and needs apply for on-premise transformation as well but the cloud with the rapid new business process package enablement generally accelerates the dynamics around it.

A classic OCM topic is business and IT alignment. Historically, many on-premise projects were described as IT initiatives without adequate business involvement. Ironically, with more software decisions heading toward use of cloud there is a tendency for the business organization to drive the decision without involvement of the IT organization. Often this is driven by the way the system and user interface are presented and sold. Omitting IT in the decision is an internal customer alignment of business with IT problem and can be a costly mistake, e.g., most of the time, only the IT organization understands the required integration scenarios to the existing systems.

Another change management topic for a business that is transitioning their ERP technology from on-premise to the cloud will be how to address the changes in their sustainment organization (CoE). How to transition your CoE team to a new model is a significant organizational change and opportunity. A number of roles within your support organization will no longer be needed as the infrastructure and technology upgrade process is simplified. New roles will be required to effectively manage the cloud software supplier and what is likely to be a more rapid pace of package software feature changes and enhancements for adoption by the business.

Supplier Management

There are typically multiple suppliers that you engage for your packaged application project. You typically start with the packaged application software supplier, some experienced consultants to help your team through the implementation and possibly an infrastructure hosting partner or cloud arrangement. There are multiple facets of partnering with these suppliers. For example, the packaged application software supplier in addition to providing the software, will have software consultants and a support team that you will work with. I will share some background and insight on these relationships and managing the suppliers. The figure below provides an overview of the supplier management discussion.

Supplier Management Overview

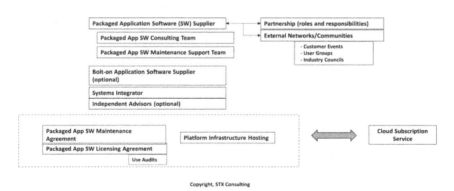

Copyright, STX Consulting

Figure 7 - Supplier Management Overview

Packaged Application Software Supplier(s)

It is likely you already have some ERP package running in your business. At some point, your software package supplier was chosen, and the right due diligence exercised and key criteria assessed to determine the best selection for the business. The decision may have been aided with some outside advisory consulting. Criteria used included customer references and proven successes with similar business processes, how easily the requirements and needs can be met (refer to business case), geography scope, usability, architecture fit, top to top relationships and cost/value/risks.

Once in place, due to the investment, the ingrained nature of complex ERP processes and the cost and effort to change, even if change is considered, customers usually continue with the initial package selection, even if effectively having to do an extensive upgrade to the next generation product in the family. I have noticed that, in general, with smaller and medium businesses, many have used out-of-the-box software for cost reasons, and this allows them a little more flexibility in their decision options in subsequent years. Cloud capabilities are enabling even greater flexibility in decision options with the rapid nature of standing up a new landscape and migrating a legacy ERP over. That said, change management still looms large when you undertake this change so the cost/value/risk analysis must be compelling to change suppliers.

Whether it be SAP, Oracle, Salesforce, Workday, Infor, Microsoft or some other ERP/application supplier, the governance of the supplier is a key to your overall value realization equation. Note that in some cases, it is necessary to include a bolt-on software application to your ERP project to fill a requirement gap. These bolt-on software suppliers need to be governed under the same game rules as well.

Your business may already have formalized pieces of supplier management software in place. These supplier management systems offer some level of governance over the ERP software supplier but are not usually focused on the project implementation and rollout aspect. The project and operational governance aspect is the piece we will discuss here. Having some advisory consulting role familiar with the supplier engagement model to augment your team can really help you make the right calls and identify opportunities to improve.

SAP is the largest ERP and business application supplier today. All of the packaged application suppliers can be an excellent partner in launching their solution whether it be on-premise or cloud but, like all supplier partners, they also need to be governed effectively in order to make sure you are realizing the expected benefits. Each software supplier offers a variety of services from standard consulting to added hand-holding support services and many other services. These services often come at a premium and can be very valuable but also pricey. Like all external engagements, a Best Practice is to keep track of the skills and services engaged and regularly track the value these are delivering. You should continually be asking yourself and the supplier, "Am I getting commensurate value from this investment and how can we improve?" As part of the supplier regular executive readouts, make sure the vendor quantifies the value they are delivering with each workstream reviewed.

Coaching Moment: The notion that a company must implement the latest and greatest software out there to be successful is a mistake. There are many horror stories of customers who were on the bleeding edge of technology. In general, a release that is stable and meets your business needs is likely a good fit for you to choose. Make sure when you check the similar references to your business that those customers are running software at or near the release that you plan to install and understand if any differences are material. There is enough other risk associated with an ERP implementation that any risk you can take off the table will be beneficial. It is also likely that the benefits your business realizes from going with the less risky software is nearly equivalent in the business case to any bleeding edge consideration. Make sure to do the business case due diligence. Being a first adopter, in addition to the increased risk, always costs more money due to additional time and resources.

If you are really compelled to go with one of the new releases of a product for some critical business need or you have decided to partner with the vendor to co-develop an offering specifically for a niche segment in your industry, make sure you have the application supplier fully in the boat with you. This should be based on a top to top relationship between your company and the supplier. Make sure you fully understand if the offering will be productized and supported through normal channels or you are getting a one-off solution that they will try to market to others but effectively you

are the only one using it from the start so you have to pay for this in the support model you are offered. You need to also fully understand intellectual property (IP) terms and who will own what as usually the supplier won't agree with the project unless they get full access to resell the IP. The net here is, make sure you are fully aware of the pluses and minuses, whether it is a bleeding-edge release, or you are looking to create a very unique competitive advantage by partnering with the application supplier. I have been involved with both scenarios. Bleeding-edge initiatives can serve a purpose. Co-development efforts are much more complicated. Having an experienced independent advisor to advise in this scenario can be a good approach since it is such a one-off scenario.

Packaged Application Software Supplier Partnership

Managing and maintaining KPI information on the partnership you have with the packaged application vendor to assist you in making the best decisions is a Best Practice. Clients that create (customized) dashboards with the data they need and include it in regular status calls with their suppliers are in a better position to effectively manage their partnership. Some of the packaged application suppliers are also responding to this need by providing tools that aid in consolidating key data for their customers to view and use routinely. For example, SAP recently introduced a program, "SAP for Me", to provide a consolidation point of key supplier relationship data for their customers. The goal is to provide a new customer portal for its customers, and its vision is to become the digital companion of anybody at the customer who has any kind of interaction with SAP. Not a Sales portal or an SAP.com business portal but more of "how you engage with them" portal. Data includes what software you have licensed, what incidents you have raised with the vendor, the account management team members and so on.

Vendor portals like this are a great service to the customer. You just need to make sure that the data available meets all of your needs. It is likely that you will need to augment what is being provided with data which is only available from your side of the relationship. Things that you track (or should track) to have a more complete view of your supplier. After all, the packaged software and supplier is instrumental to your business so having a comprehensive view of the relationship and how you are engaged will enhance governance and makes good business sense.

Understanding Your Packaged Application Software Provider Engagement Roles

As part of your supplier relationship, it is valuable to understand who you are working with from the supplier, their role and relationship with you and what motivates them. Most packaged application software suppliers have similar structure and engagements models, from Sales to Consulting Services to Support to other specialized services. These role names may change depending on your packaged software supplier, but you will have an account <u>sales</u> representative whose goal is to aid you in understanding the product offerings and manage that relationship with you and your company.

From the global support team, they will work with you on any on-going <u>support</u> (your maintenance agreement), technology issues and even offer special incremental maintenance hand-holding services as needed. These special hand-holding services are usually an annual service to which you subscribe. The services are designed to do preventive and proactive maintenance as a main objective. The service also behaves like an "insurance policy" to assure you get top class help when the project is on fire.

The software supplier <u>consulting</u> team is focused on providing professional consulting services. It is not unusual that even if you have an outside systems integration consulting team, e.g., Accenture, EY, that you augment that effort with a few packaged supplier premium consultants to have the software supplier fully engaged and held accountable for an aspect of the solution implementation. A consulting manager will work with you to oversee consulting.

If you have specialized <u>custom development</u> and innovation needs and projects, most suppliers also have a way to support you with this work, likely a dedicated unit within their team. For example, if it is critical to your business to have some custom extension to a standard module, this team would engage with you in collaboration to undertake this. (In general, it is prudent to avoid custom co-development as it drives up project and support costs significantly, so it is critical to clearly define the business case for this type of effort.)

If you are a large enough organization, packaged application software suppliers may dedicate a <u>global account director</u> to oversee all aspects of the relationship. These directors are responsible for keeping you moving forward with your investment and keeping aligned with your strategy and needs.

Software Supplier User Groups and Influence Councils – Another aspect of optimizing your packaged application investment is joining global user groups and their local sub-teams. We will use SAP as an example, but all software suppliers should have user groups. Some suppliers have a larger installed base and therefore, they have larger and more topic specific focused user groups. For example, ASUG is the Americas SAP Users Group and DSAG is the German speaking SAP Users Group. These groups meet annually at the global SAP customer event SAPPHIRE in collaboration with SAP and have other meetings. There are many country/region specific user groups. Within these country user groups, like ASUG, there are regional groups that draw the user groups together three to four times a year to network, have users share lessons learned and to learn about new offerings from SAP and its partners, e.g., the ASUG Carolinas User Group. There is also SUGEN, the SAP User Group Executive Network, a collection of members from around the globe with a goal to speak to SAP collectively as one group about broad common needs.

In addition to the user groups, there are industry and process councils that work closely with SAP to help influence the product offerings. For example, the SAP High Tech Executive Advisory Council, works closely with SAP to influence product development to better reflect the on-going High Tech industry demands.

You really need to take advantage of a Best Practice and have some representation from your company's ERP community participate actively in the appropriate user groups and councils to learn from others, share knowledge and influence the product direction. Having the ability to speak with other customers who have "been there and done that", share lessons learned and the opportunity to get a regular updated view of supplier product and solution roadmaps, is invaluable. These customer exchanges are one of the most effective ways to network, learn and improve while bolstering your overall company's own community knowledge base via internal readouts and lunch and learn briefings from participants of these user groups and councils.

Packaged Application Software Licensing

You should be doing a regular value analysis on your packaged application software. Find out where the (ERP) packaged software fits in to determine which modules do not add value and which do. Licensing is a key criteria IT departments and business teams need to get right to improve the return on investment of the software. Incorrect licensing can be costly and may reverse any potential return on investment from your packaged software implementation. Just do an internet search on "ERP Licensing issues" to get a glimpse of the types of licensing troubles that might lurk out there. Because of related incorrect licensing, the legal system ruled that one customer had to pay approximately 70M USD for the unlicensed use of ERP application data being interfaced with their Salesforce application.

Many businesses also continue to buy licenses and fail to reuse licenses. Regularly review your enterprise software agreements. Confirm that the users licensed to use the ERP software are still at your company. This should be done annually at a minimum and more frequently if you are nearing the license user limit. This also highlights a coaching moment. A common global boarding and off-boarding user process across the business and IT landscape should be in place. I have seen some companies where even a year or two after an employee has left, their user IDs are still visible. This is a financial and business controls issue that proper processes and procedures should resolve.

Among the issues businesses should be wary of when trying to maximize their packaged application software investment is that the suppliers may offer tempting software bundle deals, which include extra modules either free or heavily discounted. This can be especially true of on-premise software packages. The software supplier salesman might try to convince you and your business colleagues into purchasing extra modules for a variety of reasons. The business may never use all or any of these modules. However, these modules may still incur an annual maintenance charge, even if they remain unused. This is an example of "shelf-ware" issues, purchasing software you never use and incurring related on-going expenses. Fortunately, cloud solutions typically mitigate this and provide greater flexibility to truly purchase only the software that you require at any given point in time.

I often see that businesses that purchase software packages don't seem to follow software asset management Best Practices very well. With the growth of software-as-a-service models in the enterprise, software asset managers and/or the PMO should start to look at their software as a service subscription on a quarterly basis as they treat it more like a utility fee. Apptio offers a solution for managing SaaS.

Coaching Moment: Keep track of named users. Don't overpay for users you don't use and (re)negotiate your contract accordingly. Software often falls under an End User License Agreement (EULA). If your contract is already in place, you will need a renegotiating trigger where you and the supplier are in discussion over a new license use and that is an opportunity to explore adjustments to the agreement. Once again, cloud EULAs are more likely to be structured for on demand module and user count needs but it is still worth noting as a point for the agreement review and sign off.

Consider software license specifics when developing the total cost of ownership (TCO) and business case. Subtle license elements can wreak havoc on a business case. For example, understand your ERP indirect license use policy and access to its ERP data from interfaces from external applications like Salesforce, Workday or some other package. Requiring incremental licensing costs (and annual maintenance fees) for this data access if excluded from a business case can add a significant cost to the equation and jeopardize the overall ROI. Some customers feel like this "licensing gap" is effectively double charging them for what they already have licensed once so it is much better to clearly understand these contractual details and catch this up front rather than be surprised by it down the road.

The comprehensive licensing policies of the ERP vendors certainly need to be considered if you are a new customer looking into ERP packages. If you already have a user-based EULA in place and you need to extend it for your third party interface architecture, bundle it with some other licensing agreement that you are engaging upon. For example, vendors often require a software license upgrade when they require you to upgrade their package to their next generation offering, e.g., ECC to S/4. You may receive some credit for the old software license, but it is usually modest. Software supplier deals always get sweeter at quarter end and especially at fiscal year-end. If you are fortunate enough to be in a situation where you are still determining your packaged supplier and price is a factor, like any other negotiation, leverage the purchase timing to your advantage. If relevant for your business future, you should include specific terms for divestitures and acquisitions. This includes being able to reduce the number of users and terms to address operating the divested business during the transition period (1 to 2 years is not unreasonable).

Additionally, the impetus for upgrading to the new technology may not be new function the business requires but rather that the old software will run out of standard maintenance support by the supplier. There are a couple avenues to explore here. First, actively engage with the user groups to find customers who share your sentiment and engage collectively with the supplier in open discussions on the topic. By getting the software supplier to extend the standard maintenance end of life date further out, you buy your company more time to plan and make strategic decisions regarding use of the software package. You can also explore custom maintenance contracts with the software supplier to provide support for their legacy offerings which you continue to use until the timing is right to move forward.

The good news on this specific topic, as more and more packaged software becomes consumed via the cloud versus on-premise, it diminishes some of these software end of life and support issues (but always a good question to ask your software supplier). It does introduce its own set of issues related to cloud and license subscriptions. For example, cloud licensing requires a much bigger focus on penalties than on-premise licensing. This applies to the service level agreements (SLAs) and unavailability of the productive system as well as the other test or development systems and platforms.

Packaged Application Software License Use Audits

Software suppliers may audit your use of their software to determine if you are operating within the guidelines of the license. The audit is likely more of an "event" to the on-premise discussion vs the cloud, but regardless, it is important that you proactively know how you are using the supplier software. The supplier will typically have some type of audit policy where they automatically assess what software is being used at some regular frequency, e.g., annually. It is a Best Practice to have your CoE, PMO or other relevant team do a voluntary self-assessment regularly and based upon that, take the appropriate action. The software vendors often provide tools that allow the customer to perform self-assessments. The audit is for assessing your contract and legal agreement with the supplier and usually involves a very significant amount of money, so manage it that way. There are typically clauses in these agreements that the supplier can effectively shut down your operations for violating the license usage.

With cloud, and depending on the supplier, there is typically a common license use view as part of your online account, and you can view relevant metrics consumed versus what is licensed under the subscription. You should have someone on your team be responsible for managing your cloud account with the supplier to regularly monitor it to see what has been consumed, if it looks accurate and if you need to start planning for increasing (or decreasing) your subscription.

Manage your license contract including user licenses across your company and not within individual business units or organizations. This will allow maximum flexibility for reuse of licenses. In companies with a large number of users, the time and effort to do active user management can be significant and has to be planned.

Packaged Application Software Support

There are many aspects to post-production support. The processes, the governance, the tools, the organizational structure (centralized, distributed, a bit of both….). Having architected and managed one of the largest CoEs in the world for a large IT company as well as worked with numerous customers on their support models, setting up your support model is dependent on a number of items. My goal here is to share a high-level view of that support model.

The solution support approach for your packaged software application will vary depending on the size of your company, processes and geographies in scope, on-premise, cloud, hybrid infrastructure basis, organization culture and several other factors. Regardless of the scenario and even if you outsource all technical support aspects, it is to your benefit, and I would suggest, essential, to have some application business knowledge in-house to support issues and questions that arise from the business. These skills will be key to you capturing the value from the expensive package implementation that you are undertaking. Many customers refer to their packaged application support team as their center of expertise (CoE) for the packaged based solution. There are many Best Practices that surround developing that application support team but one lesson that is a must is to start thinking about your needed support early and at the same time as you start planning for the implementation. Without the proper advanced planning for support, you could find your company going live with the packaged software without the required skills to support the solution after the external implementation consultants complete the implementation stabilization and typically move on. Retaining those external consultants for a prolonged period to support your solution post go-live can get very expensive and only exacerbates the need to get your in-house team ramped up to speed.

Coaching Moment: By starting the support planning early in the project cycle, you can incorporate a knowledge transition plan within the implementation activities to assure that knowledge and Best Practices are transferred from your external consultants to your in-house team. This assures that you begin to transition the packaged application knowledge from the external consultants with enough time and activities to do a thorough knowledge transition.

Packaged Application Software Support Licensing Annual Maintenance Costs

The annual maintenance costs can add up very quickly for on-premise licensed software (vs subscription services), given the large number of applications in an ERP vendor's portfolio. It is vital to have a clear view of the annual maintenance costs and how they will be funded. A Best Practice is to allocate the total costs across the business. Allocating across the business achieves an effective process at rewarding those businesses who have embraced the enterprise move to a packaged application while taxing units who do not embrace it. Poor governance models around the maintenance license costs can turn into hot potato discussions, especially as internal instance mergers take place. I experienced one company that recovered costs by allocating an amount out to each line of business instance owner annually by taking the total maintenance cost and dividing it by the number of instances across the enterprise. This was often referred to by the business owners as the "tin cupping" approach to cover the enterprise software license maintenance agreement. Several of the business unit teams would make this process painful for the central ERP governance team trying to recover the funding to pay the vendor. Combine that "tin cupping" model with system instance consolidation or ERP sunsets, resulting in the recovery amount increasing due to fewer business units using the software, and this turned into each unit pushing back. Ultimately, the enterprise still had to pay the vendor the same amount for its annual enterprise maintenance bill, but it didn't matter to the individual business units who saw their "allocated tin cup" amount go up. The net here, allocate at the tops of the business to drive the desired enterprise behavior via the governance model! (To make this story even more entertaining, in a few of the cases where an ERP system was sunset, the individual business team was claiming the "savings of an ERP license", though the company still had to pay the same full annual maintenance amount. To take this story one step further, one of the "ERP sunsets" was reverting back to a "legacy ERP" system, to "save the costs of their enterprise ERP allocation". To say the enterprise governance at this company was lacking would be an understatement!)

Along with software licenses, businesses should also collect metrics on their ERP support. This should cover not only the volume of support calls, but also the complexity of the support query and how quickly it was resolved correctly the first time. Such metrics can be useful when renegotiating an ERP maintenance contract or evaluating third-party support providers. Software vendors are getting much better at supporting their software and providing a more accurate view of their performance, but it is still worth keeping an eye on. Cloud platforms where patches and updates are applied automatically by the supplier may reduce the number of software support issues, but it still warrants assessing the need to keep your view of how well and how timely your supplier is addressing your reported support problems.

Packaged Application Software User Experience (UX) and Usability (Ease of use)

A technology area that is quite critical to the success of user adoption is the user experience and usability (ease of use) of the package software. The reputation of many ERPs is of being reliable, but difficult and complex to use. In the past, enterprises often limited their investments in ERP user experience (UX) testing/validation figuring users could learn to use whatever software was put in front of them with enough training and no other choice. This didn't always turn out well. This "forced adoption" approach however is changing. Employee expectations around UX have changed drastically, driven by the infusion of consumer web designs in enterprise software, smart phone apps and cloud-based browser access. For example, most ERP suppliers have rolled out new user experience strategies that include mobility support. There are some estimates that state that up to 70% of interactions with ERPs system could be via a mobile device so having a good user experience solution here is paramount.

User Experiences will continue to evolve with technology. Voice augmented systems where AI input is provided to assist and guide the user is underway. Augmented Reality (AR) is already being used for service technicians as a way to guide them to troubleshoot the problem and resolve. For example, Microsoft HoloLens AR/VR is being used by technicians in guiding them to facilitate the on-site repair process.

Super users/key users/power users, which we described earlier as key enablers of change within your company, should engage the end users early on to assess the usability of the solution by the end user community. Ensure the usability assessment is done with realistic data volumes. Without realistic data, initial usability experiences may be good but later on in production when the user has long response times between steps the negative experiences will surface quickly. Usability is a very important criteria to be assessed by the project team to help qualify the level of resistance that might be experienced. Depending on how easy it is to use and how intuitive the solution is, the business can better determine how much and what kind of end user training may be needed. I have seen many projects not assess the ease of use factor of a solution early, only to realize at go-live that some key process task turn-around times will take months to stabilize to a point that is close to what the business was achieving with the previous legacy solution, which everyone had become accustomed to and familiar with using.

There are many examples of poor user experiences being responsible for the lack of use and adoption by the user community. The CRM marketplace and its history prove the importance of user experiences. The software suppliers that have had easier to-use-and-adopt software have had a history of success. Early on, when CRM first started to make its presence known, Siebel CRM was able to successfully enter the market against the larger ERP vendors selling CRM solutions because, among other factors, users saw it as easier to use. Salesforce with its CRM cloud offerings has resonated very well with customers in this way.

There are many negative consequences and examples of where a non-user-friendly interface hampers the user experience and value. In the ERP space, which seems to have more than its fair share of less than ideal intuitive interfaces, one of the software suppliers was essentially requiring solution implementation be managed out of its own solution management software. The related user environment was highly technical and far from intuitive for the general project leadership and executive team to navigate. As a result, project data was not viewed in real time and was typically extracted into spreadsheets and PowerPoint presentations for the weekly project reviews with the executives. This made it difficult for the project leadership to get an accurate and timely overall view of the implementation status. The resulting lack of timely and transparent project implementation data played a contributing role in a number of key implementation misses and delays. The solution implementation software was too complex to use and effectively limited the leadership team from viewing the data that would have been most beneficial. The parsed abbreviated weekly reports often were intentionally trimmed by the respective individual team leads to present a more favorable picture of how the implementation was going versus what was actually happening. The overall leadership and executive team never questioned the fact that the data they were viewing was not timely nor truly accurate for their implementation project. This ease of use issue combined with other governance challenges contributed to the large project being late and being millions of dollars over budget.

Enterprises have also woken up to the intangible costs of ignoring UX such as alienating employees, adding to the workload, creating process fatigue and encouraging 'shadow IT'. 'Shadow IT' is the IT activity that creeps up within a business without any real plan and often built by others outside of IT. It drives additional costs for development and support that are not captured. Governance needs to address it.

Coaching Moment - Plan for better user experiences and usability. Prototyping and simple user interface walk-throughs performed early-on in the preparatory and design phase can save months of issues on implementation and even be the difference between widespread business adoption or widespread business resistance to the solution being implemented. A solution can be functionally elegant but if it lacks the ability of the users to understand and use it, it will be a guaranteed painful experience. One client I spoke with shared that they experienced a doubling of cycle times to get finished product out the door as the warehouse users found the new solution overly complex with two to three times the number of transactions required compared to the legacy solution. It took almost a year to turn this situation around through process and ease of use changes and even then, as a result of the bad experience, the users did not feel like they were implementing the best solution to benefit the company.

As part of the user experience metrics, it is critical to fully understand process execution cycle times before and after implementation. Though not always an "apples to apples" comparison, if the new process cycle times are much longer for similar processes, this highlights the need to assess further transformation analysis. Is added process simplification needed or is it the complexity of using the software or an end user training issue or something else. Simple cycle time analysis during solution testing is an activity that might help shed light on your to-be processes and help you proactively address these issues and mitigate risk before going live.

Systems Integrator (SI)

It is common to use a systems integrator to assist with your effort. This is a crucial partnership and you need a good partner to work with. Unless your company is one of the few that has all of these internal skills and expertise, you will need to select an SI partner. Regardless, even if you have the skills, at some point you will need to engage an SI or external consultant to augment your team with hands on implementation experience of a newly introduced offering. You should go through an SI selection process and decide based on defined criteria. It is important that you choose the best fit SI because they will be instrumental in helping lead you through the efforts to implement and support the solution. Key SI selection criteria include top to top relationships, customer references and proven successes with similar scaled engagements your business regions, deep organizational change management expertise, chemistry fit with your culture, and cost/value/risks.

A systems integrator often brings their own methodology into the engagement. These methodologies are all built on top of the application supplier's methodology with tweaks that the SI has added based on lessons learned and IP they have developed through past experiences. The software application supplier's methodology is typically very good and well documented.

It is important for you to understand what players you are getting from the SI you have chosen. Explicitly ask, "who will be the main interaction point for day to day activities and provide the expertise"? Ask to approve consultants that will join the team, confirm they have the skills you need and don't hesitate to roll them off if they don't. Make sure you are not being sold the 'A' team but getting the 'C' team. Inventory the skills that are joining the team and keep active track of planned and actual roll off dates. Agree on how they will manage and communicate timelines and budgets. Include travel and living (T&L) costs in your monitoring because these costs can often be very sizeable and the further the distance consultants travel into your site the more likely they will be delayed or need to leave early to return home. Remember, these are the consultants that are supposed to transition knowledge to your team to make your team self-sufficient. Ask the SI for an explicit transition plan, specific deliverables and metrics to assure your team is becoming self-sufficient.

One of the key responsibilities of the SI consultants is to help you design the solution and map your business rules into the capabilities of the packaged application, often referred to as "configuring the application". Ideally, you will be able to use all standard configuration. With cloud offerings, packaged software suppliers are striving for more and more of a standard industry configuration to serve your needs by continually enhancing product features, though they support customizing as well. Standard cloud offerings have benefits and drawbacks. Benefits include no customizations, faster rollout of new enhancements and likely lower costs to operate. The drawbacks include how best to incorporate capabilities that are differentiating into the standard offering and the related long-term support. Small to mid-size businesses often strive for the standard configuration.

The SI configures your business rules into the packaged application plus refines and loads your master data, e.g., products, customers, vendors, to effectively enable your business processes within the application. Any customization or modifications required to satisfy needed (key differentiating) business capabilities that were identified as design gaps must be scrutinized and judiciously assessed with strong governance before inclusion in the solution. This customization in ERP is enabled via Workflow, Reports, Interfaces, Conversions, Enhancements and Forms (WRICEFs). The fewer the WRICEFs the lower your cost of implementation and on-going support. Your SI should play a strong advisory role with your governance body to determine what gets added to this WRICEF list. The WRICEF list should be actively governed and viewed as an opportunity to be managed for simplification. For example, determine which custom code (WRICEFs) has been used by the business in running business transactions within the last year and if not, can the code be removed. Note that with the advances in analytics and business intelligence and ease of use, custom reports are getting displaced by query tools to be used by the end user. More on analytics later.

Independent Advisor(s)

Some companies augment their team with an independent advisor(s), either as member of the PMO or to separately advise the executive steering committee or project executive or just to come in to assess the program at a key junction point. These independent advisors have no affiliation with the SI or packaged application vendor. The SIs are usually not fond of any independent view of their work and will often position to the client that it is not beneficial, stating that they can govern themselves. However, these independent advisors are usually very seasoned consultants with many implementations under their belt and experience either working for an SI or the packaged application software consulting team, e.g., STX Consulting. They can typically be engaged part time and participate in a regular cadence with the client. They can also be brought in for "red team" reviews when things are bumpy in the project and you may need an independent set of eyes to assess and provide input. Having a trusted independent advisor adds benefit to your overall program governance model. This advisory knowledge can radically improve your decisions and results. Given the typical ERP implementation costs, the business impact and a ten to twenty-year operational life of the solution, it can be well worth it.

I have observed situations where customer executives blindly embrace the SI advice resulting in very poor outcomes. This issue is amplified when project executives have no previous experience or knowledge of ERP projects. The void results in the selected project executive creating a "blind" dependence with the SI, rarely questioning guidance. This has derailed more than one project. In situations like these, it may be the executive steering committee or champion that engages the independent advisory consultant.

Unless your project or implementation is in a state of euphoria, bringing in an advisory consultant for a several-day independent assessment can be very beneficial. Whether you are in the middle of your implementation, in the post implementation operation phase, you have a large Big Four SI or you are tackling the project with a local boutique consulting firm, having an independent expert to bounce things off can provide a validation point for key workstreams. The cost is small and the potential upside great. If you were undertaking a major home re-architecting and felt unsure of some advice or the path you were on, you would likely bring in an independent advisor, so why not do the same when you are re-architecting your business with ERP?

Advisory roles can also extend to more prominent independent advisory firms like Gartner and Forrester. These firms provide insight into many areas of packaged application. Keeping in mind that these are not typically implementers but rather firms that work with a broad collection of clients and vendors and synthesize the data they gather from the market and customers into independent analysis for consumption. This information is often invaluable as a data point.

Infrastructure and Development Operations
We discussed technology platform infrastructure earlier in the chapter. I would be remiss if I didn't at least introduce "Dev Ops". Combining your **development** with your infrastructure **operations** (Dev Ops) efforts for increased efficiencies and improved software delivery is an avenue to explore for opportunity, if not yet done. Applications and tools for governing your infrastructure and Dev Ops are essential to finding and extracting added value. ServiceNow is probably the most familiar application provider of tools to manage and analyze the respective data from infrastructure and Dev Ops. Additionally, using process mining technology for better visibility on the processes you execute for your infrastructure and software development, whether within the ERP toolset, within packaged applications like ServiceNow or from your outsourcing provider, will provide the increased insight you need to easily govern and optimize those services processes.

Interfaces
An area of your packaged application software implementation that often introduces significant challenges in most landscapes is that of interfaces between the new applications and the legacy applications. I have been engaged in numerous projects where the interfaces are not functioning correctly and causing immense negative impact to the project. One client had major problems with their third party logistics (3PL) provider interfaces and since the shipping process was all outsourced, this caused major shipment issues with their customer orders. As part of a critical situation (crit-sit) team called in to help stabilize the situation, we had to do significant root cause analysis on the issues before resolving and rebuilding the business team's and customer's confidence in the ability to rely on that interface. It also required a sizeable interim manual process until the issues were resolved.

Interfaces can be the bane of ERP projects and any packaged application implementation. The more application interfaces required to function with your packaged application software the more likely one of those interfaces will not work correctly at some point. Ideally, when designing the solution, strive for fewer application interfaces and simplify the interfaces that are required. Develop a comprehensive approach at managing and governing interfaces that includes analyzing interface designs, incorporating the interface into the end to end process analysis, identifying control points, developing internal agreements between the business application owners on how issues are resolved and clear ownership roles. Business process owners should be actively involved in governing interfaces in their respective process areas. Dashboards should include key data on each interface. Interfaces will fail and as Murphy's law dictates, when it fails, it will be at critical times or when nobody is available, like a holiday weekend.

Technology Governance

It takes all three parties, the packaged application supplier, the systems integrator, and you, the customer, working together to be truly successful and win as one team. All three teams have equal responsibility. Everyone needs to play their best and governance, communications and collaboration are key skills.

All of the technology governance aspects discussed in this chapter need to be monitored. These aspects include the software, infrastructure, technical consulting, partners, supplier support and methodologies to implement the packaged application solution and operate it. Key performance indicators identified by the business need to be qualified and quantified to best monitor how well the Technology pillar is operating.

For example:
- Software Supplier Management
  o Enterprise costs
  o Software licenses, contracts and general business awareness of what is licensed.
  o Incident management
  o Additional maintenance agreements and support contracts, e.g., Max Attention.

- o Use of software supplier consultants
- o Functional enhancement requests to suppliers for their packaged application
- o Participation in software supplier user groups
- o Participation in software supplier customer industry advisory councils
- SI Management and Transition Planning (identify required skills for self-sufficiency)
  - o Enterprise costs
  - o Plan targets
  - o Resource skill mapping
  - o Resource T&L cost monitoring and management
  - o Target roll off dates and related transition plans
  - o Knowledge transfer monitoring
  - o Transition planning as a workstream starting with the initial project plan
- Cloud Provider (Infrastructure Hosting)
  - o Enterprise costs
  - o Service Level Agreements
    - Downtime monitoring and analysis
  - o Incident management

Cloud solution technology has greatly facilitated the implementation and governance of many aspects of the underlying packaged application technology discussed in this chapter. There is even some irony in that you can use packaged application technology to manage and govern your growing portfolio of packaged applications from SAP, Salesforce, Workday, Oracle, Infor, Microsoft and others. There are a broad range of applications that address the technology management space. From IT Management suite packages like ServiceNow to best of breed applications that address software license management, supplier management, and other point solutions. You can start small to manage your top priority items using Excel and your own business rules or a niche best of breed package or a software suite-based IT management solution and then broaden the footprint. Cloud technology makes it easy to execute in an incremental and pay as you go fashion!

One additional comment regarding technology. Many of the references in this book are for ERP applications. However, the majority of topics, Best Practices, lessons learned and coaching moments covered here are packaged application agnostic. They apply to any packaged application implementation and on-going support efforts, likely on a smaller scale than an ERP program. In addition to the technology pillar, all of these respective packaged application projects require effective organizational change management to align your business teams and stakeholders. These projects require business process ownership and accurate master data. They also need to be governed proactively.

Chapter 7 – Winning Games, Playoffs and Titles – Value Realization

"I've always believed that if you put in the work, the results will come. I don't do things half-heartedly. Because I know if I do, then I can expect half-hearted results."
Michael Jordan, 6 Time NBA World Champion

You need to plan to put in the work to achieve your goals. We have discussed multiple ways to improve your results and some are certainly hard work. In the following chapters, we build on this work with additional insight to help with your value realization.

Peter Drucker, business management guru, is credited with saying, "You can't manage what you don't measure." Though a well-worn business axiom, it holds true for driving value out of your ERP and packaged application investment. How do you know you are realizing the value you identified up front in your initial value assessment and business case? Are you measuring and monitoring the pillars that enable that value during implementation and sustainment of your packaged application? We now build on previous examples to give you better visibility, insight and management of your transformation efforts; organizational change, business processes, technology, and the overall governance applied across these pillars. If you don't put the foundational measuring, monitoring and rules in place when beginning the packaged application initiative, how can you expect the results to surface when the game is underway?

As a bookend to his earlier quote, Peter Drucker also said, "Management is doing things right, leadership is doing the right things." Below are some thoughts on those "right things" to help your program achieve value realization, success and victory.

Thoughts on Value Realization and Governance

Value realization (VR) planning and management must be naturally incorporated within the whole packaged application delivery and support life cycle methodology you are exercising. Here are a few questions to gauge your maturity on the VR process. Are you

- Assessing your as-is processes, organization and landscape to identify value realization use case opportunities?
- Identifying and quantifying the value?
- Identifying the high level to-be solution?
- Creating the business case and calculated ROIs?
- Incorporating proof of value (PoV) activities for the identified use cases to provide a high-level verification that your benefits are realistic?
- Developing the implementation roadmap with checkpoints to verify the value realization expected as you proceed through the project life cycle?
- Assuring that the value realization effort is an ongoing activity with ownership and responsibility for it built into your solution sustainment team (CoE)?
- Incorporating lessons learned into your value realization and business case development process to improve the VR model for future use case ROI calculations?

Effectively Govern the Implementation

What questions should you be asking of your team to make sure you have an effective governance model in place for your packaged application implementation and its ongoing support? You can start by checking some basics. Are you

- Following a comprehensive life cycle methodology?
- Exercising appropriate phase exit criteria?
- Regularly checking back with the business case and value assessment to confirm you are on track?
- Using a dynamic project governance dashboard to monitor key (actual) real time data of the project versus classic weekly project team scorecard reviews? This avoids viewing data that can be prepared by team leads to sail over issues with executives to avoid difficult conversations that may not always shed a positive light on the team lead's respective efforts. For example, on one very large

transformation project, one process domain leader was behind on his business process simplification analysis work and rather than call out all of the challenges, he collaborated with the technology team to pull in thousands of lines of custom code with many modifications from the legacy ERP solution to replicate the complex legacy support problem in the new "simplification" project. It is unclear if the executive leadership team ever realized what happened as that domain leader was rewarded with a promotion for meeting the schedule. In reality, the massive corporate "simplification" investment was saddled with a huge support carrying cost and the baggage is a gate to ever moving to a more standard ERP solution that can easily take advantage of all of the vendor enhancements without massive retesting, analysis and support. All because the project data being viewed by leadership was fabricated and not truly reflective of what was happening in the system.

- Verifying that you are measuring the right project metrics? For example, in the earlier example where process simplification suffered due to team lead "data doctoring", had the executive team been measuring the number of lines of custom code and modifications via a dashboard, the executives would have seen the spike in custom code that the "simplified" solution now had, resulting in an immediate addressing "the elephant in the room".
- Have you identified the right change agents to be your super users? These should be the best of the best on your team. They are at the core of driving the cultural change required within your business with the new packaged application software. Have your properly prepared them and enabled them to be successful? Do you have the right number of super users identified?

Effectively Govern the Sustainment effort

To govern the solution sustainment after go-live is critically important. As difficult, and most package implementation go-lives are, the largest part of the value realization from that significant implementation investment lies in the hands of what you and your business team do with this packaged application solution to make it hum and become a market differentiator to outpace the competition. Some questions you can ask to see if this sustainment effort is taking the shape required are:

- Do you have a defined sustainment model in place with roles and responsibilities clearly defined and staffed and an incident and change requirement processes in place to support the solution and the ability to add new business requirements to meet the on-going needs of the business?
- Is a center of excellence (CoE) approach appropriate for supporting your solution? Even if it is a cloud solution, your business requires packaged application knowledge and expertise to own and advance the packaged software. You may want to outsource the lower value support tasks, but the ongoing business process enhancements and transformation capabilities should be aligned with your business strategy. You will need expertise in your business who can make this a business process led effort. Outsourced strategic roles often lack the knowledge and passion for your business to assure the commitment needed.
- Do you have the right foundational elements in place with your packaged application solution to make it work in a reliable way and thrive?
- Do you have the master data processes lined up to assure the right customer, product, supplier, financial data, is all in place from a trusted source? If the data can't be trusted, you will be unable to drive your business value realization potentially exponentially higher through data analytics.

Effectively Govern the Business Process Transformation - Implementation and Sustainment

How do you govern the full business process transformation effort?

- Are you confirming that the process simplification you set out to transform your business toward is being achieved?
- Are processes being used as designed or are manual undocumented processes actually what are being exercised by your business?
- Are you able to see where future process transformation and simplification opportunities lie?
- Is process automation viable? Which process steps lend themselves to automation and which process steps don't and why not?
- Can you begin to see where artificial intelligence (AI) and even possibly machine learning (ML) might be applied or are you still too early in the cycle with other process challenges?
- Are the new transformational processes that you put in place being adopted by your users and if not, how do you measure this and repivot the team to move in that direction?
- Do you have a view of your Total Cost of Ownership?

Total Cost of Ownership (TCO)

Total costs of your ERP efforts are a key input into your value realization calculation. Additionally, clear visibility of ERP team skills allows the PMO and project leadership to manage them. It is essential that your management team (PMO) has real time views of the costs and consulting skills being provided along with the burn rate so that those responsible for the value realization can put plans in place to govern those costs and skills. They need to have accurate data, manage skill dependencies and address skill gaps effectively. You should also be proactively planning skills needed on your team as skill demands change over time and putting the proper plans in place allows your team to transition from its current skills state to the future skills state needed in a timely manner. I have seen ERP projects burn over a million dollars a day on large pricey consulting teams with management not really prepared to ask hard questions on value being delivered during PMO program reviews with the suppliers.

TCO is typically comprised of several categories and variable vs fixed expenses. Whether you are using homegrown tools or commercial applications to manage TCO, the data should be timely. Cost categories include external (software provider, SI provider, cloud provider…) and internal (team members, tools, supporting infrastructure….) factors. The figure below is an example for reference of some of the components that go into a TCO model. Many companies have multiple ERP implementations in place across business units.

TCO Components Example

	Implementation	Solution Sustainment
Software Supplier(s) (License or Cloud Subscription)	Software License(s) or Cloud subscription, Consulting Skills, Bolt-ons	Software License Maintenance or Cloud subscription, Consulting Skills
Systems Integrator(s)	Consulting Skills	Consulting Skills
Internal Resources	Team members, End Users engagement	Team Members (Some or all of Support could be outsourced), End Users
Infrastructure In-House or Outsourced (Cloud)	Hardware/System Software or Cloud	Hardware/System Software on going or Cloud
Other	Tools, Subcontractors	Tools, Subcontractors, Continuous Improvement Projects, Upgrades

Copyright, STX Consulting

Figure 8- Total Cost of Ownership Example

The PMO should have a very active governance handle on the ERP or packaged application TCO as it is critical to the value being realized. Additionally, once you go live with the solution, the sustainment team (CoE) should be actively tracking TCO and own the value realization responsibility.

It is common in companies with a sizeable legacy application investment for their ERP transformation project business cases to have a legacy IT application sunset benefit within the business case as well as business transformation benefits. A Best Practice across your broader IT, business process and application landscape is to have a view of the ratio you are budgeting on IT to transform and move the business forward versus the amount you have tied up in running it. ERP application implementations and footprints can consume a significant piece of the overall business process and IT landscape and costs.

Transform/Run IT budget analysis is one way to gauge overall IT performance and is a common industry benchmark. The benchmark data is generally available as some ratio of IT budget spent on these efforts as well as the overall IT budget as a percentage of revenue. What isn't spent on "run" operations should fall into the "transform" bucket. Additionally, some benchmarks also add a third bucket to this analysis associated with "innovate", which is basically spending money on changing existing solutions that you already have to add revenue. Spending an increasing percentage of your IT budget on transforming and innovating the business to move forward and a decreasing percentage on running your systems "to keep the lights on" for daily operations is a common goal and KPI. See Figure 9.

There are a number of firms that provide updated industry benchmarks on the percentage an industry is spending on IT and how they are proportionately spending it. Doing a quick internet search on "run" IT spend percentages reveals that the majority of companies operate in the 30-70%+ range of IT spend on "run" with the balance on "transform" and other improvements. That is a large range and warrants obtaining specific benchmark data on your industry. However, 30% on "run" vs 70% on "run", implies that some companies are able to direct almost twice the spend percentage on making significant changes targeted at improving the business for your customers. The goal should be to drive the "run" costs down while enabling more dollars to be applied to your "transform" and improvement causes.

You can also search IT spend as a percentage of revenue by industry, you will find that the Banking industry spends nearly 7% of their revenue on technology while the Construction industries spend less than 2%. Quantifying and measuring the business value that those invested dollars are providing in "run" vs "transform" plus "innovate" is a more qualified assessment of the IT spend percentages.

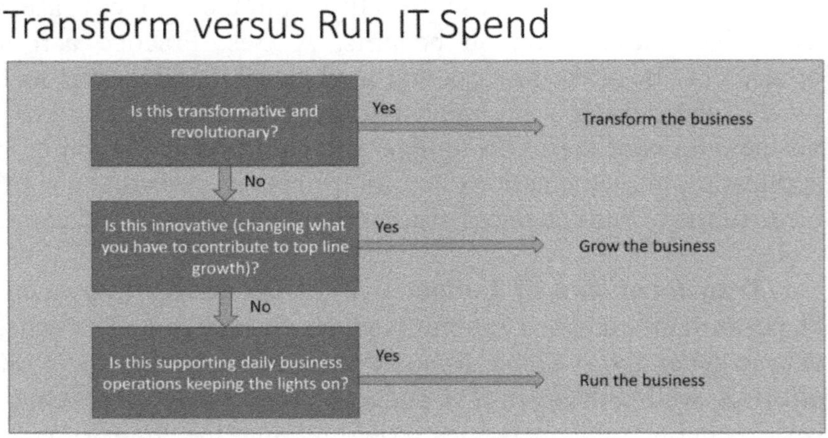

Transform versus Run IT Spend

Figure 9- Transform versus Run IT

A Best Practice is to systematically inventory all of your IT application investments, categorizing the application as "run" or "transform" and "innovate", providing a business process classification and any other categorization that adds to the desired analysis. This application inventory is typically part of the overall enterprise architecture team's responsibility and they work with the process owners to make sure the data is accurate. The "application maps" are typically viewed as "heat maps" to show where the largest investments and opportunities are and help in identifying candidates for sunset and inclusion in ERP and packaged application business cases. By tracking by business process, process owners and the business team can assess if they are realizing the value and "bang for their buck". If your transformation is process led, it facilitates this analysis greatly. See Figure 10.

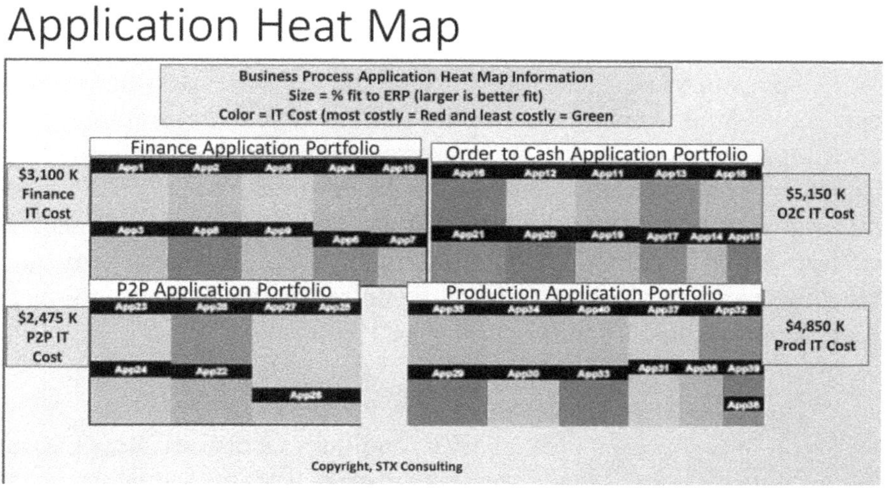

Application Heat Map

Figure 10- Example - Legacy Application Fit Heat Map to Your Packaged Application

The transition to leveraging cloud applications offers a unique cost take down opportunity and move from a capital expenditure (CAPEX) model loaded with infrastructure and software license and costs to an operating expense subscription as a service monthly/annuity basis fee. It changes many of the budget planning dynamics that the business has to contend with, e.g., large enterprise license one-time payouts and corresponding hardware purchases.

Your ERP TCO, both the one-time implementation and the on-going operations, should be actively managed under your value realization workstream that the CoE typically owns. These costs will be a significant contributor in your Enterprises overall IT spend. Applying relatively small percentage efficiency changes typically have a large impact on costs. As I shared earlier in the book, annual ERP operating costs can approach 10% or more of the ERP implementation costs. I have seen implementation costs in the 1-3% of revenue realm, so these overall costs are significant, regardless of the size of your company. Likewise, applying small percentage efficiency changes to the business processes enabled by your ERP system, will result in a relatively large value increase. When all of your sales orders flow through your ERP application (all of your revenue), improving "days sales outstanding" (DSO) or reducing billing delays has a large upside to your value equation.

Later, we will discuss how through the use of process mining, you can reduce the demands on your ERP technical programming and consulting resources and free up resources to be applied to the transform and innovate side of the house for greater value. The process mining features and capabilities will also likely reduce ERP package customization demands and by minimizing those, it will make it easier for your business to adopt more of the newer features and functions the ERP supplier is introducing in their ERP offering.

Go-Live and Hypercare

You have used your go-live readiness decision checklist and everything indicated the risk of a go-live was manageable, so the decision was made to proceed and go-live.

Coaching Moment: Don't make the serious mistake of disregarding the readiness input from your team and the decision checklist facts, e.g., testing still has major outstanding bugs, users are clamoring that the training was woefully insufficient. Ignoring the facts and going live with the house on fire and your team scrambling with readiness is a telltale disaster sign. I was called into a critical situation (crit-sit) scenario after go-live with one client where the decision to go-live was clearly the wrong decision. The major integrator that they were working with obviously failed them and didn't provide the quantitative and qualitative metrics and advice that should have delayed the decision. The client spent nearly 10 months trying to stabilize the global business and global transformation effort, lost a number of major customers and many key client team members got burnt out and left. Fortunately, my team was able to help the client to stabilize critical customer facing processes and after several months, the client was able to get nearly all of the customers to return.

Hypercare is the term applied to that period immediately after go-live where everything truly is hyper. It is the first time the new to-be processes are being exercised. The business is on edge as even minor issues can cause disruptions to key customer support efforts. The hypercare period is when the entire team including the external consulting team, your super users, the on-going support team (CoE) and your business team and end users are all ramping up, executing the new processes to run the business. The "happy path" of business processes that people plan for are often fine but when the real-world deviates from this "happy path", proper preparation can mitigate the impact and even make it a non-event. However, most companies don't plan for many of these one-off scenarios and Murphy's Law always dictates they have a higher probability of occurring during critical times. Your preparation should have included how to address these one-offs when they do arise so at least you are procedurally ready. The number of process variants off the "happy path" can be eye opening even to the most seasoned leaders. Process mining tools can open your eyes to the number of process variants your business really operates as part of the project preparation and process simplification analysis. More on process mining later.

Coaching Moment: Properly prepare to support the solution after go-live, including hypercare planning and making sure you have the right level of skills on board to provide business as usual support through your CoE. A Best Practice in transitioning from hypercare to "business-as-usual" is a set of well documented criteria that the business process owners use to define that the to-be processes truly are stable and the business is comfortable transitioning to a "business-as-usual" operate world where your CoE is now in charge of providing support. This criteria list should be developed and agreed upon as part of the go-live readiness checklist.

The following hypercare exit criteria example figure shows a matrix of key business criteria assessed on a per process basis, e.g., no open critical tickets, super users trained and ready.

Hypercare Exit Criteria example

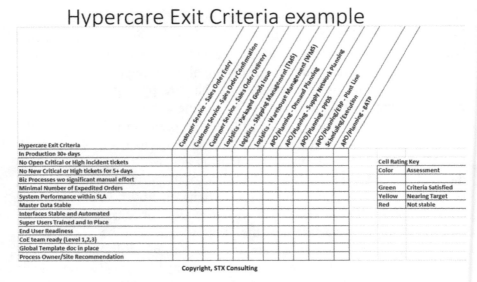

Copyright, STX Consulting

Figure 11- Criteria to Exit Hypercare and Enter Business-As-Usual Phase

Thriving in Solution Sustainment with a CoE

A key reason implementations fail to deliver on expectations is because a company believes it is done at the go-live date. That is far from the truth. The go-live is just the beginning. It may seem like the weight of the world has been lifted by going live but the hard work of keeping the business running and moving forward still exists. Also, extracting the value from the sizeable packaged application implementation investment should now be front of mind for many executives who signed up for the business case and are now looking for their investment to pay off. You also need to think about talent retention and new hire boarding and training as part of this mission. Most methodologies now include the "how to set up" the "run/operate" phase of the ERP packaged application implementation. There are many things that go into building a best in class CoE able to support the business and the ERP live footprint. Skills, effectively replicating required skillsets from your implementation since you have to sustain all of the same technology and organizational change; processes, both incidents and new function (ITIL and Dev Ops), supplier management, tools (productivity and operations), and infrastructure, which is a larger element for on-premise. Setting up a CoE organization and processes to drive optimizing your investment going forward is hard work. There are many Best Practices around the sizeable tasks that are critical to success One of them is starting early in the project planning phase and another is to leverage an advisory consultant who has done it before.

Stability and Beyond

Once your business is satisfied that the hypercare criteria are met and the solution is stable, the team can transition to the final phase of the project and operate the solution in a business-as-usual model. Keeping in mind that this SHOULD be the time that (a) you emphasize driving the value realization effort (b) you incorporate in your metrics measuring the value realization regularly and perform root cause analysis if not on track and (c) work with your business team to look for additional opportunities to get even greater value from your significant packaged application implementation investment. As mentioned earlier, super users are in a unique position to drive added ideas for improvements with their pre-existing business process knowledge combined with the packaged application knowledge they acquired as part of the implementation team. In Chapter 8, I elaborate on ways to further optimize your solution for operational excellence and additional unplanned benefits for years to come.

ERP Value Realization Examples

Some examples of large transformation initiatives which can be leveraged under the value realization umbrella: (1) common global process enablement, (2) business process transformation across multiple business processes, (3) transform/run spend improvements, (4) an empowered workforce and (5) application of effective analytics and AI on accurate and timely process and master data that results from your ERP implementation. Further elaborating on these value realization examples:

1. Common Global Processes

    –   Shared services, e.g., customer service, payables

- Consistent (superior) customer experience, e.g., customer service, invoicing

- Drive greater synergies

- Enable faster merger, acquisition and divestiture process transitioning for faster ROI and adaption to market changes

2. **Business Process Transformation**

   - Process productivity enhancements, e.g., days sales outstanding, collections, supply chain

     • Enable seamless supply chain paths through inhouse production or subcontracting, to more quickly satisfy customer demands and increase agility

     • Third party drop ship process enablement and visibility of the end to end supply chain, including component inventory at your suppliers

     • Enhance logistics, procurement timing, and inventory distribution across warehouses and stores

     • Improve complex manufacturing processes and resource allocation to reduce bottlenecks and cycle time

   - Standardize/outsource non-differentiating processes

   - More easily model/simulate process changes or a new process

   - Continuous improvement process (CIP)

3. Transform/Innovate/Run Spend Ratios

Sunset multiple legacy applications - Legacy IT sunset and "shadow IT" elimination/reduction to allow the local business teams to more effectively get the work done versus struggling with complex solutions.

- Better equipped to shift more spending from "run" to "transform"

- Leverage cloud and SaaS to enable rapid adaptation to market changes via adoption of new technology and processes

4. An Empowered Workforce

- Employee growth and empowerment opportunities which aid in enhancing the organizational culture.

5. Better and Easier Data to Analyze

- Customer, product, supplier, sales, supply chain, finance data analysis

- An enabler for additional market differentiation and digital transformation

- Use of process mining and AI to provide fully transparent processes which then enable Best in Class optimized processes and customer experiences.

- Benefits can be realized across supply chain, customer service and profitability, financial performance, HR, quality management, production, plant maintenance and R&D.

Each of these value realization examples would be accompanied by associated key performance indicators aligned to your strategy which can be monitored and managed to assure that your business goals are met or exceeded.

Coaching Moment: The foundation of powerful data analytics capabilities for your business are both quality master data and ERP plus packaged applications where business processes run effectively and data footprints are created for every aspect of your business. Without the quality master data and quality ERP solutions, there is no source of data to mine or the data is corrupt, unreliable and of limited value. Garbage In = Garbage Out.

Data is now a critical corporate asset. It comes from the web, business applications, billions of phones, sensors (IOT), payment systems, cameras, and a huge array of other sources—and its value is tied to its ultimate use. While data itself is becoming increasingly commoditized, value will accrue to the owners and players that can aggregate the data in unique ways to uncover hidden data-gems.

Getting ERP right helps to make your processes transparent. The more visible and open you can make these systems within your business, the easier it is for different teams across the organization to optimize their related processes and realize value. Process mining is well suited to help you reach the prerequisite data analytics elements of quality master data and effective ERP and packaged application process transparency. This can help your organization behave with a process improvement mindset. It is game changing to be able to quickly identify and address your process issues that are gating improvements to satisfy customers. As I shared earlier, process-centric led transformation can be found in organizations that are industry leaders dictating the rules of engagement. We have discussed many levers to improve your ERP packaged application outcome and achieve the goals upon which you planned. Which levers you apply and when to accomplish your business success depends on your unique situation. Next, we will talk about building on that success and taking your game and company to the next level.

Chapter 8 – Your Legacy, Establishing a Dynasty – Years of Growing Satisfaction

"Perfection is not attainable. But if we chase perfection, we can catch excellence. "

Vince Lombardi – Legendary Coach of the Green Bay Packers, winning 5 Championships in 7 years.

We are aware of dynasties in sports. The Green Bay Packers when Vince Lombardi won 5 Championships in 7 years; The New York Yankees dynasties among their 27 total World Series Championships and many legendary names; Michael Jordan's Chicago Bulls who won 6 championship rings; The Montreal Canadians of the 1970s and their four consecutive Stanley Cups. These dynasty runs can last up to a decade or longer where teams consistently perform at the pinnacle of greatness year over year. It takes great individuals, great collaboration and great coaching and leadership for teams to consistently operate with excellence for dynasties to be born.

Continuous Improvement and Innovation Culture

Ultimately "winning the game" and building a business dynasty, that is, enjoying many years of business success from your ERP and packaged applications, is about keeping your customers satisfied and continuing to innovate to stay ahead of the competition. Success with your customers includes understanding customers' needs as opposed to customer wants. Making sure you understand what your customer truly needs is not always easy. Henry Ford stated, "if we'd have asked the customers what they want they would have said faster horses". We do know we need to be agile and adept at adapting to be able to respond to changing demands quickly.

At the core of your business strategy and goals is keeping the customer happy. As Sam Walton, the founder of Walmart, a business team with many years of success, said, "There is only one boss. The customer. And he can fire everybody in the company from the chairman on down, simply by spending his money somewhere else." Being able to pivot quickly to changing customer needs, reinforces your requirements for business agility and adaptability. Packaged application software can provide for rapid adoption of new technology and processes for greater agility. Effective and timely package adoption starts with the need to implement effective change management, business processes and technology.

Reaching and then maintaining your competitive edge goes hand in hand with innovation and good ideas. This means creating an environment of innovation. ERP projects should be an opportunity for driving cultural change. In the book, "Where Good Ideas Come From", the author, Steven Johnson, lays out multiple examples of creating environments for continuous adaption, improvement and innovation. For example, he discusses how Liquid Networks were essential to "Building 20" idea generation at MIT. Building 20 was a hotbed of idea generation and was instrumental in many intellectual achievements such as highspeed photography, single antennae radar and the development of the physics behind microwaves. The building was constructed quickly from plywood as an extension to the Radiation Lab at MIT to aid the Allies in WWII. It was notoriously hard to navigate resulting in unplanned collaborations between lab groups within the building. The wood stud walls covered by plywood also allowed the researchers to quickly reset the internal layout to suit whatever needs they had. The building collaboration traits highlight the collaboration that packaged application projects require and why team "war rooms" are such an effective way to achieve cross business function communications during ERP implementations. The cross functional ERP team communications that happen in a "war room" is critical given the many integration points in ERP packages across different business groups, e.g., Finance, Supply Chain, Customer Service, HR, Master Data.... You need to leverage this cross-team collaboration into an on-going cultural mindset. Continue to nurture it and don't let it stop with the go-live.

This highlights the need for creatively establishing team collaboration communities with the ERP go-live to continue the idea development. Technology available through teaming, collaboration and social networking solutions, e.g., Microsoft Teams, Slack, Zoom, Webex, YouTube... can be leveraged to establish and nurture user communities led by your super users, process owners and CoE.

Establishing your continuous improvement and innovation culture is essential to driving operational excellence.

Coaching Moment - Building a community and social network from business stakeholders, to process owners to super users to end users and external partners, establishing an open and collaborative communication platform and culture is a Best Practice that the Best in Class companies have been able to put in place and enhance. They also take advantage of external networks. They have team members participate in the packaged application supplier user groups and industry councils as an additional forum for learning and sharing insight. They always look for opportunities to learn and grow and extend their network and idea base.

Data Analytics

A recent analysis published by the World Economic Forum estimates that the entire world has more than 44 zettabytes (44,000 exabytes or 44,000,000 terabytes) of data, and that volume is projected to double every three years.

Data is the new corporate asset class and the best way for companies to generate and access it is to digitize everything they do. Digitizing customer interactions provides a wealth of information for marketing, sales, and product development, while internal digitization generates data that can be used to optimize operations and improve productivity. All of the ERP package suppliers offer business intelligence (BI) and analytics options. Since data abounds within businesses from many sources, customers also have chosen to apply a variety of analytics and visualization packages to these data pools and warehouses, e.g., Tableau, Splunk, Qlik, Microsoft Power BI, Celonis…

Recent advances in data analytics are now making possible even more improvements to the packaged application solutions customers have in place. Empowering your teams to drive the on-going value realization with data analytics will help those teams to clearly understand what is happening to your business and existing processes. It can also help identify where the best opportunities lie and how best to address these opportunities with guidance from artificial intelligence

(AI) algorithms operating on the data. The volume of available data has grown exponentially, more sophisticated algorithms have been developed, and computational power and storage have steadily improved. This is all fueling rapid technology advances and faster business disruptions.

These business disruptions can involve identifying new opportunities using analytics insights to streamline internal processes and revenue streams and enabling continuous learning and feedback. Some industry leaders have developed digital models of the entire production process.

Examples of data analytics led improvements in ERP applications include incremental internal cost reduction and revenue optimization. On the cost take-out side, data can be used in predictive maintenance, talent management, procurement, and supply chain and logistics planning. On the revenue optimization side, insights from data can be used to enter new markets, target customer sub-segments, improve product features, and make distribution channels more effective.

Game Changing Analytics Examples

Sports teams have also taken advantage of the new data analytics capabilities. The movie "Moneyball" starring Brad Pitt, was about the budget challenged 2002 Oakland Athletics ascent to the pinnacle of baseball and winning the World Series by using data analytics to assess bargain players to recruit while other teams stayed away from these players.

Every professional sports team now has data analysts and data scientists on staff that they work with to look for nuggets of data to exploit for competitive advantage. This can come in the form of ways to exploit one on one match ups for the upcoming game, to improving individual player performance to who to draft. The list of opportunities is endless and teams continue to innovate. The NBA has gone as far as to track and analyze the players entire movements through the game.

An excerpt from an article by Dan Knopf, October 18, 2017, "Data analytics have made the NBA unrecognizable" from the online journal Quartz:

"The NBA has embraced statistics with a verve that may even surpass that of Major League Baseball, the first US sports league to let data into the locker room. Nearly every team in the NBA now has data analysts on their staff who work with coaches and player evaluators to maximize individual athlete's talents and identify undervalued players. Many players use wearables and sleep monitors to track their fatigue levels in order to avoid injury."

"Analytics are part and parcel of virtually everything we do now," NBA commissioner Adam Silver said at an analytics conference held by Wharton School of Business earlier this year."

These examples are evidence of data mining opportunities that go from game changing breakthrough approaches for the leaders one year to being required by all who want to compete the next year. The data mining efforts and algorithms get more advanced every year as additional data and nuances are understood and exploited. Having tools and a framework to continuously improve and upon which to collect, analyze, enhance, monitor and advance your data and processes are vital.

Data Analytics Challenges

With all of its excitement and opportunity, data analytics business adoption also has its challenges. Just like other packaged application technology it faces its own set of hurdles. Organization are struggling to become mature users of data analytics and put the right skills in place. Even though they are significantly easier to use and are directed at end users, it still requires the end users to be willing and made comfortable with using the tools. Another challenging area mentioned earlier is harmonized and common master data management across the enterprise, including established business data standards. If your data is garbage, making a mountain out of it will create a mountain of garbage.

Many of the same ERP packaged application principles shared within this book to improve results are applicable with these data analytics packages as well: organizational change management, business process transformation, technology and governance, albeit on a smaller scale. Make sure you have a clear understanding of where the value will be derived and the corresponding business case and Use Cases. Does your organization's change management align to where it needs to be? Are the executives and champions in place to support and execute their roles? Will you be using consultants to help you set up the analytics and transition the knowledge to empower your team? Have you identified the processes in scope, how they will be governed and changed based upon the analytics results? Are the processes reliable and in control with KPIs defined? Is more digital transformation required to get the data necessary to provide an accurate view? Do you have the master data required to trust your analytics results or have you not normalized the data across your enterprise? Is the analytics technology platform aligned with your data and application architecture? Is important data still trapped in legacy applications? How do you plan to institutionalize the analytics data and process into your current organization and govern its success? Are super users in place and is training planned for end users? How are you going to drive the business adoption? The questions I raised above have all been addressed in this book.

Continuous improvement combined with innovation are vital to building a winning culture within the enterprise and overcoming a number of challenges. Imagine having true and full process visibility to remove the friction from existing processes to continually improve the internal and external experiences. This process transparency can remove barriers that may directly or indirectly have a negative impact on your customer experiences with you as a supplier. Process mining has recently surfaced as a focused use of powerful data analytics to provide full process transparency. Process mining vendor Celonis has customers who have been quoted as saying that using process mining is like having an X-ray of their business processes where all of the inefficiencies are completely visible for them to spot immediately and to take action on.

Process Mining

I will focus the process mining discussion on Celonis and their Intelligent Business Cloud (IBC) solution. Gartner has identified Celonis as the market leader in process mining and most mature process mining vendor, continuing to innovate and advance their technology. One of the fathers of process mining, Professor Wil van der Aalst, published the first book on process mining in 2011 and an updated and extended version in 2016. Professor van der Aalst is Chief Scientific Advisor for Celonis.

Celonis process mining is based on an iterative continuous improvement process of four distinct pillars, Collection, Discovery Enhancement and Monitoring your business processes:

- Collection – of an event log from the packaged application processes
- Discovery – of what is really happening within the data collected about the process
- Enhancement – of the business process to optimize it
- Monitoring – of the enhancements for continuous process excellence opportunities

Celonis Process Mining Lifecycle

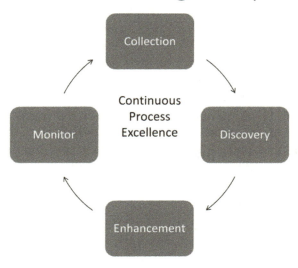

Figure 12- Celonis Process Mining Lifecycle - Adapted from the Celonis website

Process Mining Background

Using process mining to analyze your processes, find areas for simplification and introduce additional business transformation that allows improved use of the standard ERP package, can provide significant value to the organization. Process mining is a relatively new and innovative technology that is helping a growing number of companies to better understand how their existing processes are working via process analytics and artificial intelligence, proactively identifying process improvement areas. It also provides a management dashboard for monitoring the process and improvements underway. The technology is well suited to any business process that is critical to your operation where there is a relatively high volume of processing happening and increased visibility to the process would help your operations. Any business whose transformation is process led or process centric, have formal process improvement programs and teams in place or are interested in benchmarking their processes and operations, will likely be immediately enthralled when they see the process optimization capabilities that process mining enables.

What used to take an army of costly consultants weeks if not months, to come in and (partially) document your as-is and to-be process models as a one-time snapshot view, through subjective many person interviews and "sticky note" whiteboard mappings, was not effective. Add to that the fact that their enterprise ERP information systems provided no easy connection to their process world, it is no wonder that many company business leaders process management and improvement activities were struggling. But now that there can be quantitatively and objectively viewed current state processes immediately with continuous updates fed from live data through process mining and you can see the excitement reborn in the visions of those process leaders.

Process mining requires a digital footprint, which almost all packaged and custom applications offer since they are built on databases. It requires three key elements which typically exist, (1) a case or object, e.g., Sales Order, Service Order, Purchase Order, Work Order, Production Order, (2) an activity (a process step), and (3) a time stamp associated with the activity. This is effectively a digital event log. Process mining technology can aggregate these digital event logs across your company as they actually happened and continue to happen. It is creating a "digital twin" of your business in an in-memory process data engine that enables split second analysis of massive amounts of your process data. Process KPIs can be created by the analytics, measured and monitored easily. Process mining helps reduce the non-value-add activities. It also has built in cross unit benchmarking features and conformance analysis comparing outliers to the defined "happy path" process model, using AI to identify deviation root causes. Imagine the continuous improvement opportunities this opens up.

Celonis's data connection and collection architecture is also system agnostic. Therefore, their process mining tools can be applied to any packaged application that satisfies the digital footprint requirement. This includes customized ERP systems. Standard connectors already exist for the most popular packaged applications. These are used to connect to the systems and collect the digital footprint data in realtime. Your ERP or other packaged application, e.g., Salesforce, ServiceNow, can be on-premise or in the cloud. Large to mid-size companies, with several disparate ERP packaged applications across their landscape, can use process mining to provide a consistent and transparent process view across these systems that has been difficult and likely elusive to date. This can help eliminate many of the (manual) reconciliation reports in place.

Celonis has developed drag and drop tools to easily build very robust analyses. These tools include capabilities to calculate throughput across all process steps or any specific set of process steps, aggregations based upon conditions and filters, rework and with flexible date/time stamp resolution. They have also developed the Process Query Language (PQL) which is very similar to SQL but operates on business processes instead of relational databases. PQL capabilities are very powerful and include standard documented functions necessary to perform very sophisticated process analysis.

The solution also has a very powerful "Action Engine" built into it that can be easily set up to look for identified business signals and can trigger workflows, emails, webpages and guide users on system transactions, e.g., remove credit blocks that are holding up sales orders that should be released. The Action Engine is an AI powered process assistant that constantly analyzes data and sends signals based on your needs to those involved to advise them on the need to take action.

As your process mining maturity curve rises over time, there are options to take your process to the next level of continuous improvement. In addition to the AI capabilities built into the Celonis process mining solution, machine learning capabilities are also available. Built with Jupyter notebooks, the Celonis machine learning workbench integrates Python predictive models into the Celonis platform. This can be used to uncover patterns and deep root causes of friction from all the process data from across your business.

All the process mining features and capabilities discussed are available in a business user friendly and intuitive user interface. It can move much of the management and governance of the business process from a complex ERP framework to a more business friendly setting in which business executives and users feel very comfortable. What used to require technical programming and/or consulting skills and days if not weeks or months to plan and accomplish can now be performed quickly by empowered business users who are familiar with these process mining tools. It truly empowers the people who best know your business processes with the tools to make your business processes run better more quickly. It removes the complexity and mystery associated with your ERP systems and other packaged applications and turns the control back over to the business process owners and users, where it belongs!

Between the drag and drop analytics, the PQL toolbox and the "Action Engine" event and workflow capabilities, you can reduce some of your need for ERP WRICEF customizations. Instead of burying business needs in complex ERP technically developed code, business users can be empowered to satisfy business needs through the Celonis process mining standard features. Business advantages of this approach include reducing technical debt and reducing any analysis and effort required to assess and address the impact from ERP upgrades on any ERP custom code that would have been required. Additionally, process mining can be a common enabling company standard across all of your packaged applications. A common toolbox in the hands of the business users that encapsulates the underlying packaged application. It makes your team much more agile and quick to respond to business demands. That is very powerful on many fronts and a huge benefit!

There is also a Celonis content app store with a library of prebuilt connectors and business application packages with analyses, KPIs and Action Engine skills to help jumpstart projects.

Alexander Rinke, Co-Founder and Co-CEO of Celonis, often talks about removing friction from your enterprise and providing the ultimate customer experience. Celonis enables removing the friction in your business process by identifying non-conforming process activities, automating where feasible via qualified analysis and exercising process simplification due to the visibility and increased transparency into how the business processes actually work.

Given the fundamental competitive advantage process mining gives to any business, it is hard to image how any business will not be embracing it quickly or otherwise be at a significant competitive technological disadvantage. You can expect "first mover" advantages to prevail.

There are numerous articles touting the advantages of process mining and why companies should embrace it. The Celonis website has many such articles for perusing and reference.

Getting Started with Process Mining

Most companies have process challenges. A Best Practice to getting started with process mining is to focus on a key process which is package software enabled but inhibiting your strategic goals and take a "crawl/walk/run" approach. Identify the pain points from the process and confirm a digital event log is available for this process analysis, which will be used to reveal actionable root causes to your pain points against metrics/KPIs. Assess how this best fits into your organization, who can champion, who will govern, who will own and be accountable, who will execute the delivery responsibilities (analyst, business users, technical integration) and mapping roles and responsibilities. If you have a process led organization and/or ERP CoE, extending these roles should be straight forward. If not, you may need to collaborate with a senior sponsor on getting the organization aligned behind this effort first to assure successful business adoption. The size of the effort depends on the size of your business and process scope. Smaller firms often have people who wear multiple hats and can adapt to change more quickly. Process mining lends itself well to an agile approach with user involvement, iterative refinement and pareto analysis. You know your organization and culture and you know that organizational change management is vital to successful implementation. Confirm that within the plan there are tasks tied to organizational alignment, training, communications and stakeholder management. Celonis Academy provides excellent free online training for you to jumpstart your process mining team. In addition to the Celonis team, there is also a large ecosystem of partners, e.g., STX Consulting, Capgemini, KPMG, that can help augment and jumpstart your team and project.

The good news is that once your organizational alignment is in place, it doesn't take long to start seeing results. With process mining's ability to create a visualization of your processes using your own data and digital twin, it can result in developing a prioritized opportunity hit list quickly. A digital twin is not a static carbon copy. It's a dynamic representation of what's going on, synced for real-time adaptability. This pairing of the virtual and physical worlds provides the kind of insights that prevent downtime, highlight new opportunities and provide real value.

Process Mining Use Case Examples

Here is a short list of some process mining ERP use case examples and nowhere near exhaustive. Process mining is not limited to ERP and has spread into IoT, distribution networks, CRM and many other areas and packaged applications where applying increased process transparency and visibility, greatly enhances the likelihood of success and value realization. The increased value being realized can make these projects self-funding with a quick return on investment. There are webinars, YouTube videos and other documented customer testimonials that validate the industry wide enthusiasm for this technology.

-ERP Process Optimization, Complexity Reduction, Simplification and Value Realization - Identify opportunities, quantify opportunities, analyze drivers, enhance processes and monitor for continuous process improvement:

- Order to Cash (OTC) – Benefits: Improved customer delivery and satisfaction, avoid manual order changes

- Accounts Receivable – Benefits: Decrease days sales outstanding (DSO), (Working Capital-Cash), reduce delayed billings, reduce manual changes and rework
- Accounts Payable – Benefits: Avoid cash discount losses, avoid early payments (Working Capital-Cash), reduce manual changes and rework
- Procurement – Benefits: Tackle maverick buying, reduce manual changes and rework, compliance, increase sourcing flexibility and effectiveness
- Production -Benefits: Avoid unnecessary storage costs, reduce delayed completions and parts shortages, minimize rework
- Customer Field Service Management -Benefits: Improved customer satisfaction, reduced manual errors and rework, fewer field service FTEs required as a result of productivity improvements

-Master Data Management Process Improvements – From product data to customer and vendor data to other master data, process mining can provide greater transparency into the master data areas that are driving rework or manual steps. Improvements result from the directed targeted actions.

-Mergers, Acquisitions and Divestitures (MAD): Whether m**erging** or a**cquiring** businesses to grow, quickly and systematically arrive at synergistic opportunities through process mining. Benchmarking and quantifying Best Practice processes to adopt while also assessing process optimization opportunities quickly, can help you achieve the cost take out synergies upon which your merger plans were built.

Likewise, with **divestitures**, smoothing the process and organization issues by providing proactive full visibility into the processes in scope, streamline costs, reduce risk and make impossible timelines possible.

-Governance, Supplier Management and Program/Project Management: From your business process governance to change control to supplier management and program and project management, improve ERP operational process effectiveness. Driving enhanced governance, transparency and visibility is vital to a more proactive decision-making process with increasing efficiencies.

-Compliance and Controls Improvements – Providing clear visibility into processes and how and who is executing transactions is essential to improved compliance and controls. Control points can be monitored and segregation of duties (SoD) can be assessed in real time through process mining analytics.

-Value Assessment and Value Realization: Packaged application investments are significant. Identify inhibitors to value and put a plan and recommendations in place to remove those barriers. Whether it is addressing complexity or organizational change management challenges, simplifying processes or raising the business adoption rate, improve the business and IT alignment.

-Business Transformation, Blueprinting and Realization: Document the real as-is processes quickly so you can better assess the to-be needs. Leverage process mining technology to improve your to-be process design and realization.

-Business Adoption and Organizational Change Management (OCM) Inhibitors – User adoption of your ERP and packaged applications is instrumental in successful use and operation of any business process. Users can be monitored analytically through process mining and identify issues and/or inhibitors to their success. Management can better objectively understand user behavior and take action to improve it, including empowering users to self-assess their relative performance and drive user adoption and productivity.

-Support Team and Support Processes (CoE and ITSM): It is not uncommon for annual support costs to approach ten percent, or more, of the initial cost of ERP implementations. Turn unmined efficiencies into annualized savings. Uncover added value, from the initial setup of your support team, CoE and processes to assessing your current support processes, suppliers and tools.

Process Automation, RPA and Machine Learning

Industry momentum is building to use process mining as a key step for greater success in implementing robotic process automation (RPA). Industry leading analysts are pointing at future process management solutions based on process mining, RPA and machine learning. The fact that process mining is proving to be a key step for greater success in implementing RPA should not be surprising. One of the key challenges with automation is applying it to an efficient operation. Process mining tells you how efficient your process is. "Automation applied to an efficient operation will magnify the efficiency.... Automation applied to an inefficient operation will magnify the inefficiency", to quote Bill Gates and drive home the point. Adding a "winning the game" sports analogy from Michael Jordan, "You can practice shooting 8 hours a day, but if your technique is wrong, then all you become is very good at shooting the wrong way. Get the fundamentals down and the level of everything you do will rise."

Using process mining as a prerequisite to get the process fundamentals down for RPA should become a Best Practice. It will help you to determine whether the processes you are automating are the right processes and are they ready to be automated, or is there more process work required before you move to RPA.

It is expected that process mining combined with RPA and machine learning will open up incremental opportunities for process improvements and optimization. Users that aggregate data in unique ways will gain an advantage. Combining process mining with RPA is a powerful combination in analyzing and creating touchless orders. Data analytics enables faster and more evidence-based decision making. Systems enabled by machine learning can provide customer service, manage logistics, analyze maintenance records and more. As machine learning matures and associated learning algorithms evolve, problem solving will advance, including natural language processing. Organizations that are able to harness this power will see an abundance of value realization opportunities across the business.

Governance and Self-Empowerment

Analytics and process mining should play a crucial role in governing packaged application implementation and operations. These tools can be applied across all pillars of your initiative: organizational change management, business processes and master data management and technology.

The tools offer a unique capability to truly self-empower your business users. Giving them the means to improve how they perform their job, visibly see how their contributions are making a positive difference and helping the team win. This can enhance transforming your culture around continuous improvement, innovation and winning.

In the past, PMOs, project leaders and executive steering committees had to typically rely on weekly and monthly reports from the project team. That is no longer necessary. Realtime dashboards with accurate quantitative data blended with qualitative input can be presented in digestible business format and is readily available. This drives a proactive versus reactive governance. This enables implementations to be managed more effectively and opportunities for iterative improvements in on-going operations. This should result in higher satisfaction in meeting the initial business objectives and increased value realization from your ERP or packaged application investment.

Additionally, this framework enables reaching next generation benefits not even imagined or captured in the original business case. Your company and team can go beyond winning the game and establish a high level of business and customer satisfaction for years to come, greatly exceeding your original value realization expectations.

Chapter 9 – Coach's Press Conference – Wrap Up

"You can observe a lot by just watching."
Yogi Berra - Winner of 10 World Series titles as a player with the New York Yankees. As a coach, he won an American League pennant with the Yankees and a National League pennant with the New York Mets.

Watching (or listening) and learning from others is obviously beneficial, whether it be a lesson learned from something being done well or something done poorly. At press conferences, it is common for coaches to share what they have observed about the game, their team, the season and the competition. I add a few more coaching insights here as part of my coaching post-game press conference.

ERP Project History – Challenges, Lessons Learned and Other Thoughts

I started the book by sharing a question from one my customers, the CEO of the business, asking if they are the only company struggling to get value out of their ERP implementation. There are no shortages of past ERP projects upon which we can take lessons learned. If you do an internet search on "ERP project failures" one of the articles that pops up is from the CIO digital magazine, Oct 4, 2019 issue, "15 famous ERP disasters, dustups and disappointments."

Question from the press – As a Coach, how would you have better prepared to prevent those or similar failures from happening?

A number of guidelines and Best Practices shared across the chapters of this book should minimize or eliminate many of the pitfalls and risks identified in the article, other noted failures and your own related project challenges. Every company and project is unique so there is no one size fits all remedy. Below, I have elaborated on some previously shared coaching insight to address key ERP implementation and operation questions or issues. If applied effectively, these coaching notes will help your team move the ball down the field and into the value realization zone.

It would be easy to say that the root of many ERP and packaged application project disappointments was the systems integrator and/or the software supplier. However, the customer shares in the blame as well. After all, the customer is the one who chose the SI and the software package. If the customer had an effective governance model in place, it could have mitigated the situation and caught the train before it came off the rails. If the governance model was providing effective oversight of the organizational change management, process and master data management and the technology, including application and SI selection, it should have provided a view into the trouble that was percolating. There are often telltale signs of trouble brewing, e.g., integration test exit criteria being relaxed to accommodate a go-live target date with some executive handshake that it will be resolved in go-live, stakeholder and super user feedback indicating a broad lack of readiness and training, multiple re-plans with date slippages, major design gaps that don't close for months, master data conversion efforts that are significantly behind schedule. There is always risk mitigation in projects but choosing to ignore or not discern the high-risk signs and not take action to address them before moving on to the next phase of the project will result in a very poor outcome.

Some of the noted failed initiatives happened a while ago before a number of technologies matured or were available. Regardless, here are a list of related lessons to be learned:

- Large multi-instance harmonizations require a clearer understanding of the existing as-is processes. A Best Practice is to execute process mining analysis to accomplish this.
- Be careful of a "not ready but going live anyway" scenario. Except in very rare cases where there are no other options, and I understand that those do exist, e.g., divestiture deadline else exorbitant fees to be paid, if you are not ready to go live with a reasonable degree of confidence, don't go live. A very bad ERP go-live will have a much larger negative business and

team impact than postponing the project and resolving the heavy hitters.

- Being too early adopter with newly released software in the market can result in disaster.
- Inadequate design documentation without updated to-be process flows and identified control points results in a lack of good process design and maintenance of effective controls.
- Don't assume a global template that is deployed and works in a smaller business unit pilot will scale to the larger units without additional work, which could be significant.
- Program executive leadership lacking in any understanding of ERP projects is not advised as these projects are often very complex programs with many nuances, dynamics and this is a costly way to develop leadership.
- Picking the wrong SI can doom a project so qualify and do your due diligence when selecting an experienced SI. The same can be said about the packaged application software selection. Confirm early in the packaged application supplier selection process that fundamental requirements are met with the standard vendor product to avoid large customization efforts which are very high risk. Verify the software package does what you need by talking to comparable (scale) reference customers.
- Going live with not all master data migrated properly is like driving across a collapsed bridge. It is just a matter of time until your vehicle will drop into the ravine with very negative results. Master data is so critical to any packaged application that you should have multiple master data conversion/load cycles and tests to confirm the validity. Start this effort early.
- Governing the packaged application implementation of business processes after go-live is critically important to the value delivered to the business. Many companies forget that the implementation is only part of the project. Operating the solution is even more important since it will run for years as

your business platform and generate the largest part of the promised value. Better governance around the hypercare phase will lead to a smoother transition into steady state operations for the business and improve business acceptance.

- Organizational alignment, great stakeholder involvement, the right super users and a senior executive champion are needed. Organizational executive leadership and commitment to the project is essential.
- The business must fully understand its own processes and insert the best employees into the new project as Super Users. Many companies don't invest in as-is process analysis with a "why invest in the old processes" attitude and just focus on the future. That can be a mistake. Unless your current processes are absolute garbage, understanding how your critical processes run today is important in knowing how to get from current state to future state.
- Project implementation governance and scope management gaps existed with scope creep resulted in biting off too much to chew at one time and/or changing and heavily adding to the requirements half-way through the engagement.
- Process mining technology can provide significant benefits to a packaged application implementation and business use of those processes in many ways.
  o It is the best tool to drive and govern new process, e.g., O2C, P2P, FI, AP, AR, operating analysis. It helps in identifying and eliminating inefficiencies, manual effort and rework for improvement and optimization.
  o It can increase business adoption by quickly and visibly identifying areas where users may need additional training, identify efficient users to coach other team members and enable and encourage user performance improvements through visualization of team performance.
  o Process mining is a Best Practice prerequisite for any business embarking on an ERP implementation that

doesn't really understand where the key and differentiating steps are in their current process. These identified key steps are then clearly visible to be addressed objectively in future design plans.

o   It can be used to make process master data issues quickly visible and provide early signals to rectify the situation.

o   Better post go-live support processes can be enabled to resolve issues faster.

To summarize the above key lessons learned: Effective governance and executive leadership are essential, make sure you have qualified via due diligence that the software package and SI you are selecting will meet your needs, draw on targeted independent advisory expertise to improve your decision making process, strong organizational change management is required to help align business and IT, make sure the amount of scope you are implementing is in manageable chunks and you are not trying to devour the whole elephant, make sure clean master data is an emphasis, don't go live with the solution if the quantifiable and qualifiable go-live readiness indicators tell you otherwise or you have no team members ready to support the live solution, make sure to take advantage of process mining and analytics technology to document your as-is and to-be processes and use it as a powerful tool in your governance model for overall implementation and operation of the package.

Question from the press - Is Governance really that important to my business "winning the game" with our packaged application software effort and our ultimate success?

The Governance Equation

Governance can have a significant effect on the success of your efforts. As discussed throughout the book, it profoundly impacts every aspect of your transformation. Effective governance can have a multiplier effect on your people, processes, technology and packaged application project results and value realization. Poor governance can leave you short of the mark. The following figure illustrates this message.

The Governance Equation

The Better Your Governance, The Greater The Value Realized !

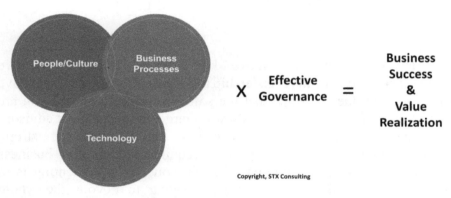

People/Culture   Business Processes   Technology   X   Effective Governance   =   Business Success & Value Realization

Copyright, STX Consulting

Figure 13- The Governance Equation

Question from the press – So if we have effective governance over our OCM, business processes and master data, and technology, we will set our team up to not only satisfy business expectations but lay the groundwork to develop future business capabilities to exceed expectations for years to come?

Closing

By exercising the Best Practices and guidelines highlighted in this book, your business team should be in a much better position to win the game and achieve the expectations originally laid out for your ERP and packaged application. You should have enabled a packaged application and business environment that (a) has established a mindset of change and innovation throughout the organization and culture with strong communications and buy-in, (b) is confident in your business process and master data management approach, (c) is using a technology platform and ecosystem built on solid partnerships that enable the business to respond rapidly to the accelerated pace of change and satisfy customers, and (d) wraps all of these transformation activities in a proactive and effective real time governance approach with transparency and accountability that leverages tools such as data analytics and process mining.

Once these foundational pillars are in place and your ERP and packaged applications are executing smoothly, your program should be on its way to satisfying expectations and winning the game. You are then ready to take your company's game to the next level. You can now build out your sound business processes and data to further leverage data analytics and process mining. Capabilities like robotic process automation and artificial intelligence can help your business significantly exceed your original expectations and mine and uncover unexpected hidden gems, wringing out even greater value for both you and your customers.

Finally, beyond those achievements, you can envision an enabled powerful, agile framework of people, business processes and technology. Your processes can be further enhanced with more sophisticated artificial intelligence and machine learning algorithms to drive value realization to heights previously not possible. Imagine new insights and business models fully enabled with predictive analytics and natural language processing on all aspects of your business processes and in meeting your customers' needs. You are driving toward operational excellence with Best in Class business processes and an organization that responds and adapts quickly. This is truly an exciting time of game changing opportunity. Don't just play the game but win the game, the title and create many years of business success!

References

American Productivity and Quality Center website, Process Classification
Framework. https://www.apqc.org/

Celonis Inc website, Process Mining, https://www.celonis.com/

Desjardins, Jeff (2019, April 17), World Economic Forum, How much data is
generated each day? https://www.weforum.org/agenda/2019/04/how-much-
data-is-generated-each-day-cf4bddf29f/

Drucker, Peter F. (2001), The Essential Drucker: In One Volume the Best of Sixty
Years of Peter Drucker's Essential Writings on Management, New York:
Harper Collins Publishers

Fruhlinger, Josh & Wailgum, Thomas (2019, October 4). CIO digital magazine, 15
famous ERP disasters, dustups and disappointments,
https://www.cio.com/article/2429865/enterprise-resource-planning-10-famous-
erp-disasters-dustups-and-disappointments.html

Hobart, Buddy & Sendek, Herb (2014), GEN Y NOW: Millennials and the
Evolution of Leadership, 2nd Edition, San Francisco: Wiley

Johnson, Steven (2010), Where Good Ideas Come From: The Natural History of
Innovation, New York: Penguin Publishing Group

Knopf, Dan (2017, October 18). Quartz online journal, Data analytics have made
the NBA unrecognizable, https://qz.com/1104922/data-analytics-have-
revolutionized-the-nba/

Wikipedia (n.d.). Operational excellence definition.
https://en.wikipedia.org/wiki/Operational_excellence

Glossary – Roster of Acronyms

AI – Artificial Intelligence

ASUG – Americas SAP Users Group

BDS – Business Data Standards

BPO – Business Process Owner

CCB – Change Control Board, the group that approves changes

CIP – Continuous Improvement Process

CoE – Center of Excellence, your solution support team.

CRM – Customer Relationship Management applications

DSAG – German Speaking SAP Users Group

ERP – Enterprise Resource Planning applications

ESC – Executive Steering Committee

EU – End User(s)

EULA – End User License Agreement (for software)

FI – Finance process

HCM – Human Capital Management applications

HR – Human Resources department

IOT – Internet of Things

IP – Intellectual Property

IT – Information Technology

KPI – Key Performance Indicator

KT – Knowledge Transfer

ITSM – Information Technology Service Management applications

MDM – Master Data Management

ML – Machine Learning

MRP – Material Requirements Planning

OCM – Organizational Change Management

O2C – Order to Cash process

PMO – The Program Management Office

P2P – Procure to Pay process

RACI – Responsible/Accountable/Consulted/Informed

ROI – Return on Investment

RPA – Robotic Process Automation

SaaS – Software as a Service

SI – Systems Integrator

SME – Subject Matter Expert

SLA – Service Level Agreement

SoD – Segregation of Duties

SU – Super User(s)

TCO – Total Cost of Ownership

UX – User Experience

VR – Value Realization

WRICEF Workflow/Report/Interface/Conversion/Enhancement/Form

Y2K – The year 2000 and related IT issues going from 1999 to 2000

www.ingramcontent.com/pod-product-compliance
Lightning Source LLC
Chambersburg PA
CBHW051244050326
40689CB00007B/1060